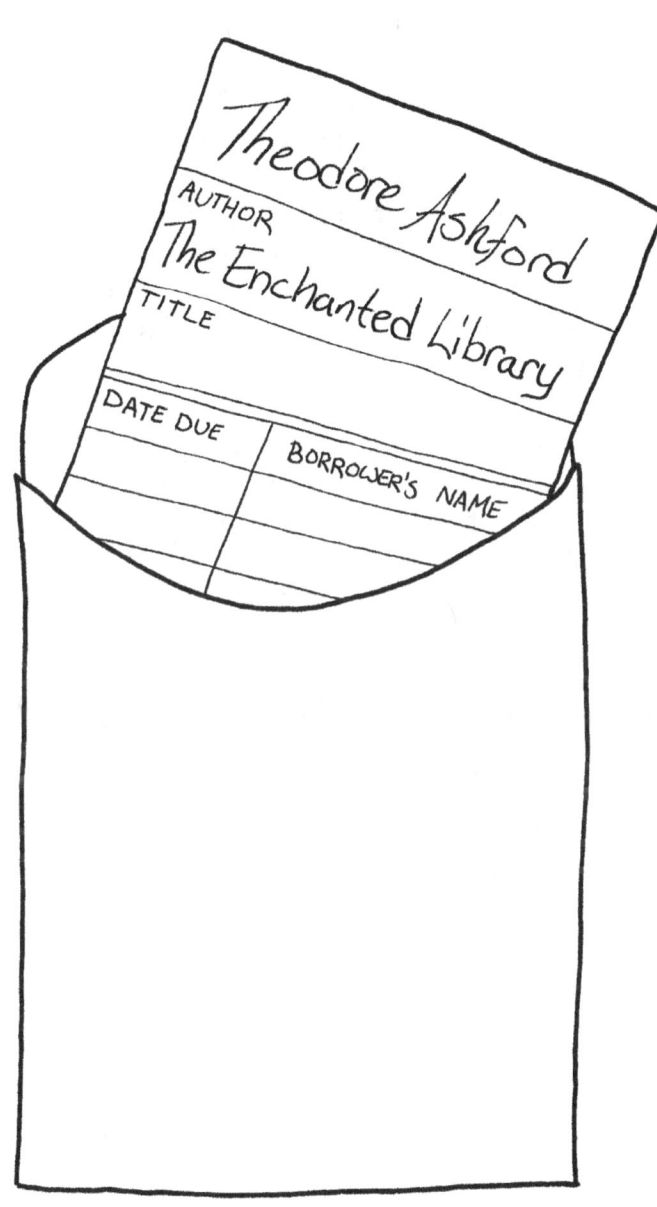

The Enchanted Library by Theodore Ashford
www.etsy.com/shop/childhoodtwopointoh
www.theodoreashford.com

© 2017 Theodore Ashford

This work is licensed under a Creative Commons Attribution-NonCommercial-ShareAlike 4.0 International License. https://creativecommons.org/licenses/by-nc-sa/4.0/

This means that you are free to share (copy and redistribute the material in any medium or format) and adapt (remix, transform, and build upon the material), under the following terms: You must give appropriate credit, provide a link to the license, and indicate if changes were made. You may do so in any reasonable manner, but not in any way that suggests the licensor endorses you or your use. You may not use the material for commercial purposes. If you remix, transform, or build upon the material, you must distribute your contributions under the same license as the original. You may not apply legal terms or technological measures that legally restrict others from doing anything the license permits.

You do not have to comply with the license for elements of the material in the public domain or where your use is permitted by an applicable exception or limitation. No warranties are given. The license may not give you all of the permissions necessary for your intended use. For example, other rights such as publicity, privacy, or moral rights may limit how you use the material.

ISBN-13: 978-1976482946
ISBN-10: 1976482941

First Edition

Interior designed by Theodore Ashford
Cover design by Ashwords Design

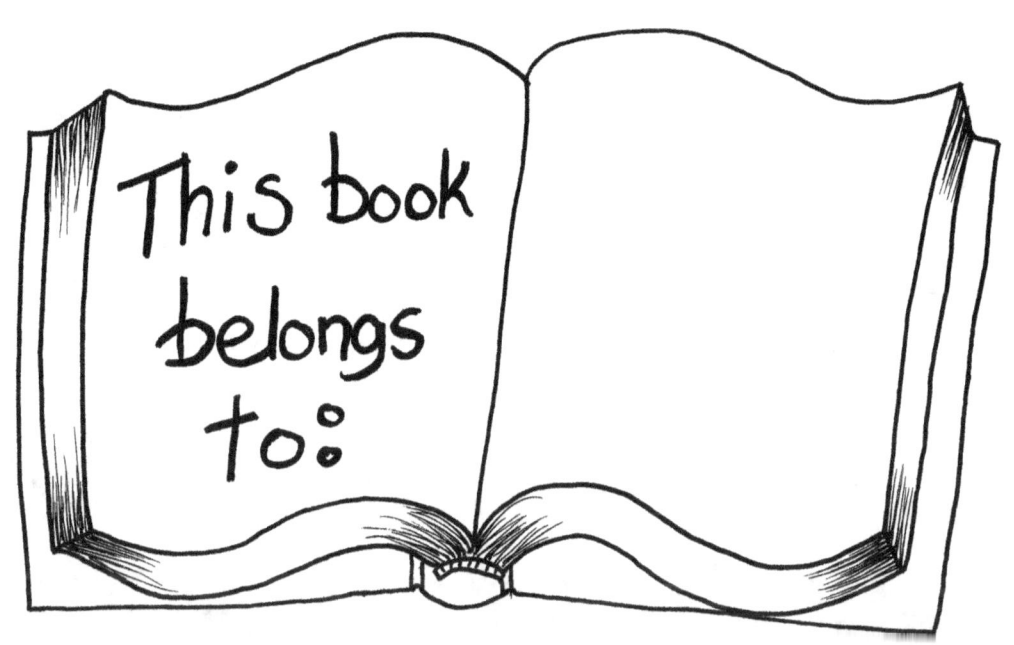

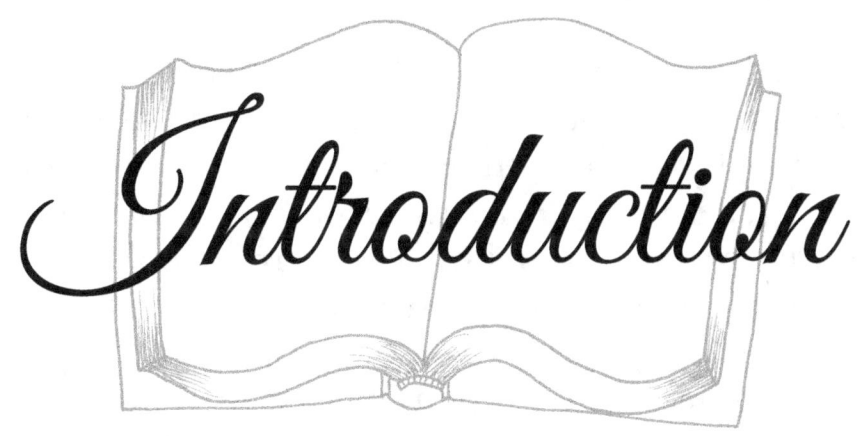

Introduction

Books are in my blood.

I've been reading since the age I could hold a book. But then again, I had a librarian for a grandmother and two bookworms for parents, so I suppose it's only natural that I grew up getting addicted to books.

When I was in elementary school, I used to spend countless nights staying up late with a book (despite my mother's protesting). Books were a special kind of magic that intoxicated me. I desperately wished for the kind of adventure that happened to my favorite heroes to happen to me. I felt like I lived in a constant state of frustration with this world. I didn't have access to the same magic as in my books, and nothing interesting ever seemed to happen in my world.

As I moved into my teen years, my book cravings started getting more and more precise, until eventually I found myself wanting stories so specific that I couldn't find any book to satisfy the craving. So I started writing my own stories instead, and got intoxicated all over again. Instead of being dependant on someone else's ideas and imagination, I could create a world that was perfectly tailored to what I loved.

I got persuaded into trying the event known as National Novel Writing Month, or NaNoWriMo. If you haven't heard of it before, NaNoWriMo is an event that happens every November where writers try to write a 50,000 word novel in one month. At the time, I'd had a problem with constantly picking up and putting down story ideas as quickly as they came to me. I'd never dedicated a full 50,000 words to any one novel before.

I ended up managing to meet the 50k goal that first year, even though I hadn't finished my novel. It was the most I had ever written at once, and I fell in love with the event. I've done NaNoWriMo faithfully every year since, whether I managed to win or not.

Then last year, I found myself in the midst of a very stressful November. Life was hitting me harder than I had expected that year, but I wanted to stick with NaNoWriMo no matter what. Writing is one of the ways I see hope in the world, and I felt like the world would get that much darker if I gave up on my writing. What I really wanted was something that could be a stress reliever for me while also reminding me of the magic in books and inspiring me to get back to my writing. Except these two things rarely ever seemed to coincide. I had many great stress relief methods at my disposal, but hardly any of them had anything to do with writing or books. There were also plenty of ways for me to get inspiration for my writing, but most of these activities weren't necessarily stress relieving, even if they were fun.

It was during one of these evenings where I searched for this perfect activity that I expressed to my spouse in a fit of frustration "I wish I had a book coloring book!" It seemed like a silly idea at the time, but the more I thought on it, the more it seemed like exactly the kind of book I wanted. I tried hunting for one online, but came up with nothing. So I did the same thing that had propelled me into writing in the first place and decided to create the exact book I wanted. It's taken me nearly a year to work up the courage to actually complete this book, but I finally managed to finish it.

The Enchanted Library is based off a childhood fantasy of mine. A library where you could spend all day there without anyone yelling at you. A library stuffed to the brim with books, and where magic spills out of the books and into the library itself. A library where there's always an oversized armchair and hot beverage waiting for you. This library was the place I liked to go to in my mind whenever the world got to be too much, and now I would like to open the library to the public.

Some days, you may just need a day to take care of yourself and try to relieve some stress, and as wonderful as writing and books are, sometimes the words may end up running away at the first sign of stress. But books have always been that safe place for me. I don't want to leave them just because I need to spend a day recovering from the world outside of books. That's what The Enchanted Library is there for.

I may not spend my days pining after the worlds in my books anymore (well, at least, I don't spend as many days pining), but I still believe in the magic of books. Books have a special kind of magic unlike anything else. I believe that storytelling is this world's version of a magic system. We use stories to influence each other, create change, to grow, to communicate. It's hard to find things that a good story can't do. Other worlds have levitation or elves or talking animals, and we have the magical ability to see into all these other worlds just with a spell weaved out of words.

I hope the magic of the stories within this library give you a chance to take a break from the rest of the world and reconnect with the child inside you who still believes magic is real and can easily spend all day curled up with a book. The Enchanted Library will always be there to be a safe place for that child.

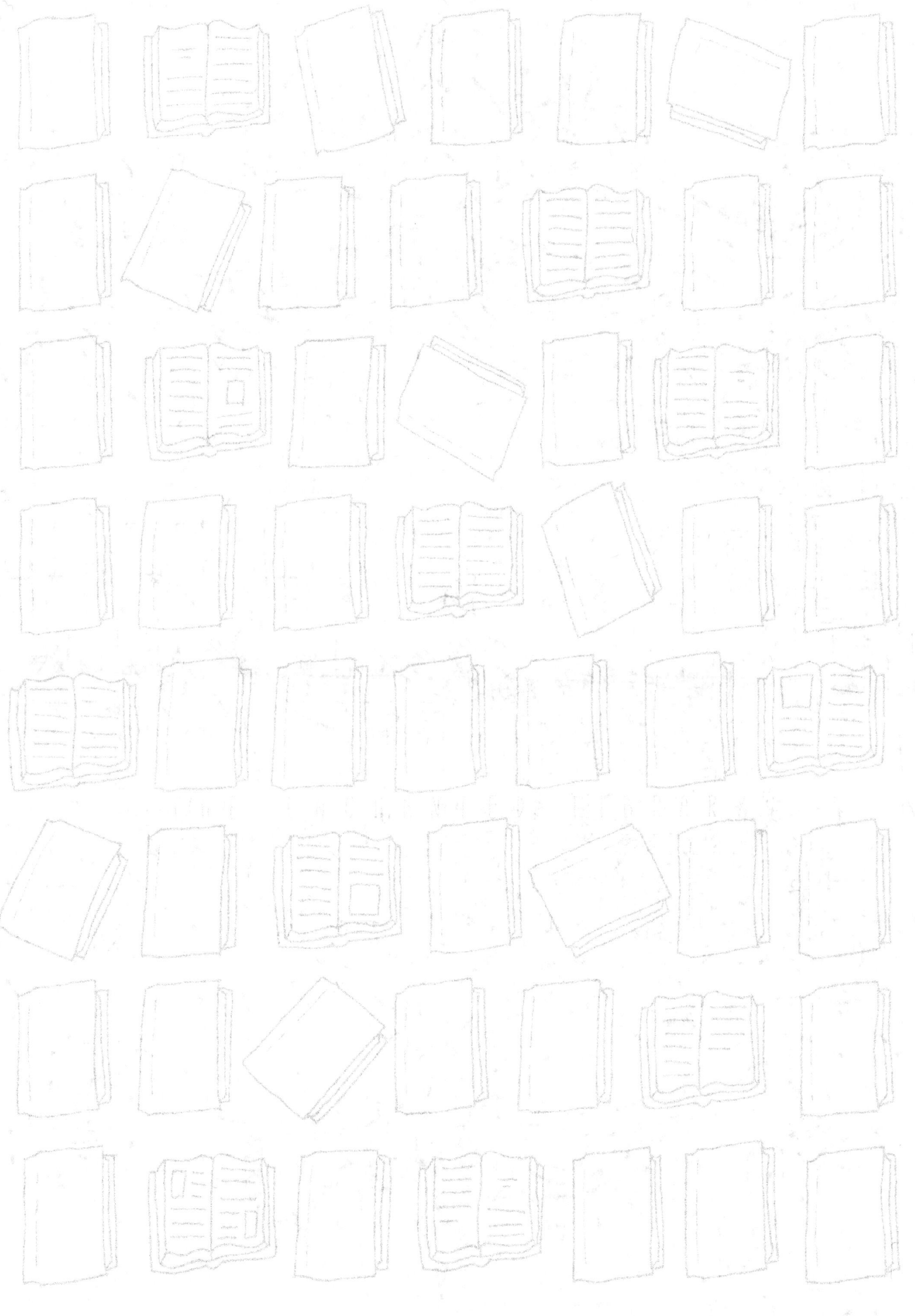

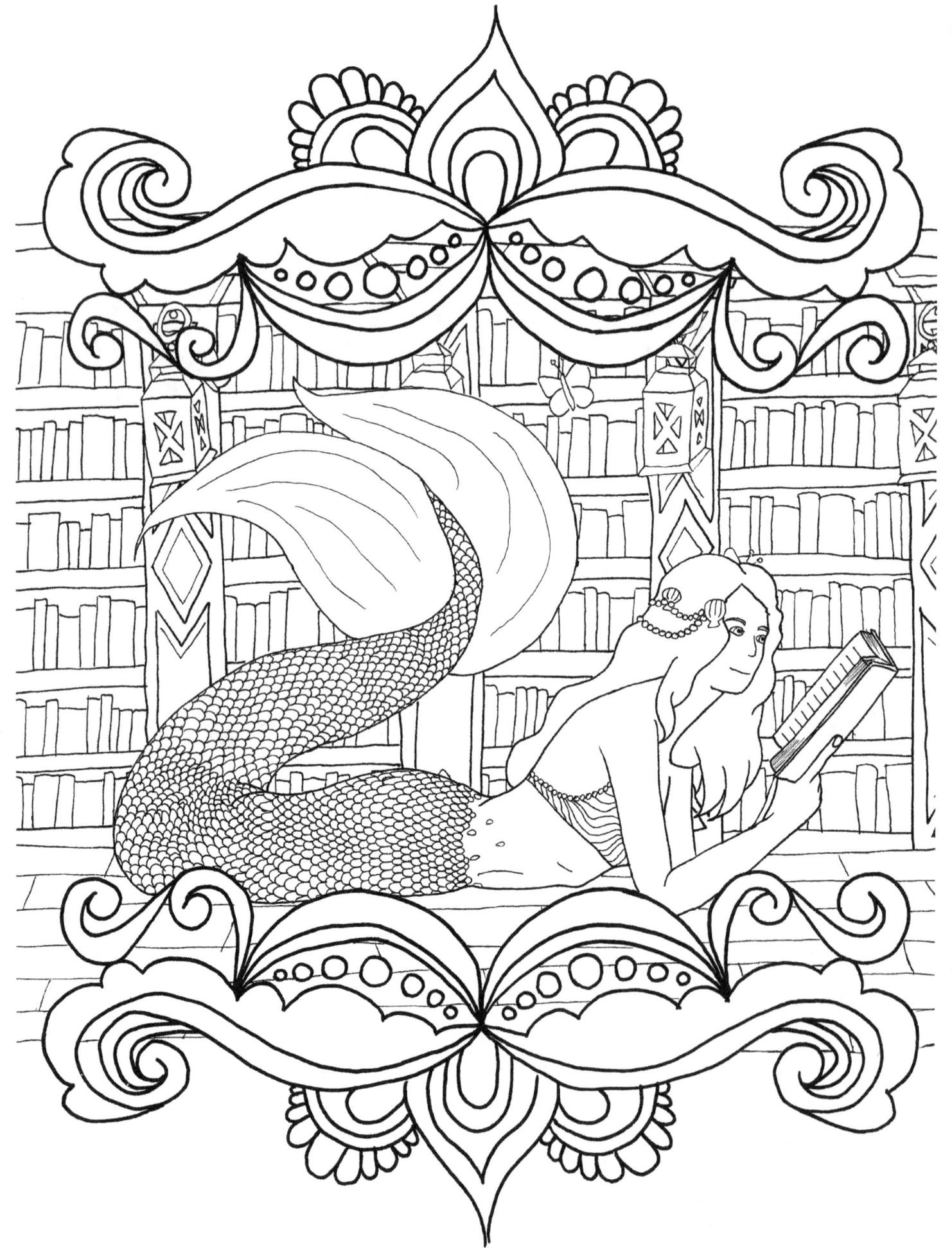

Once upon a time, there was an enchanted library, a blessed place for readers and writers everywhere to take solitude...

...And find adventure.

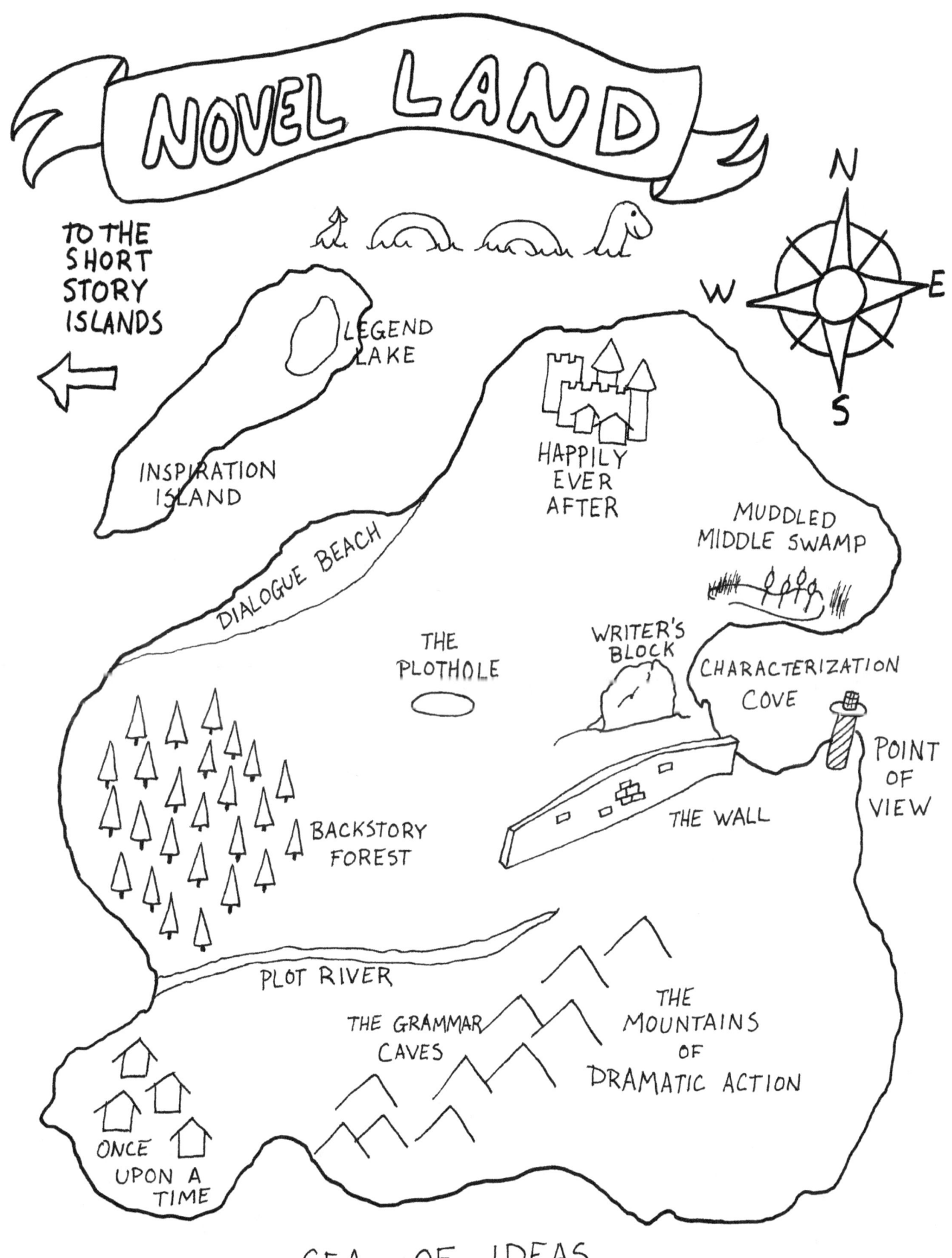

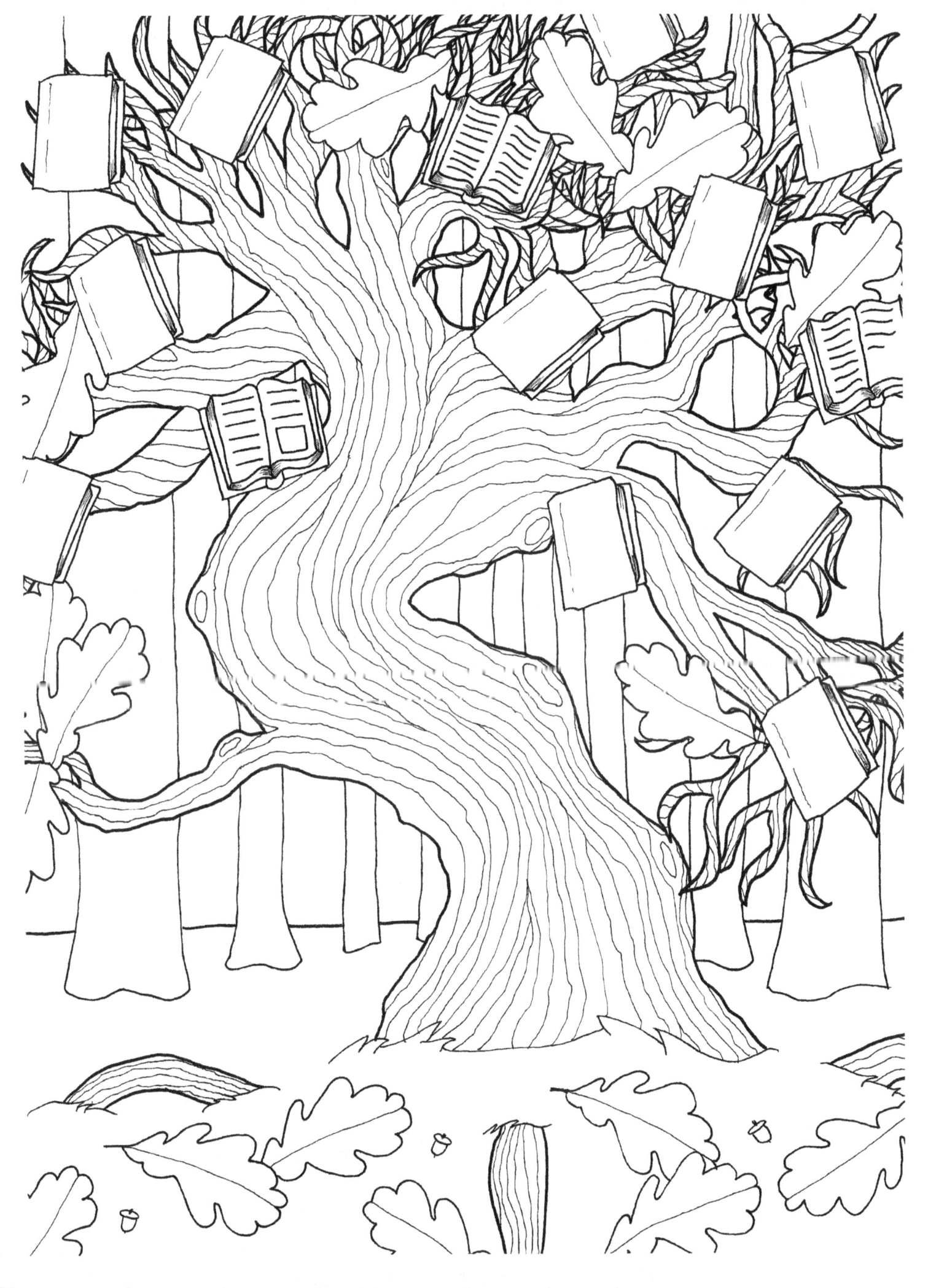

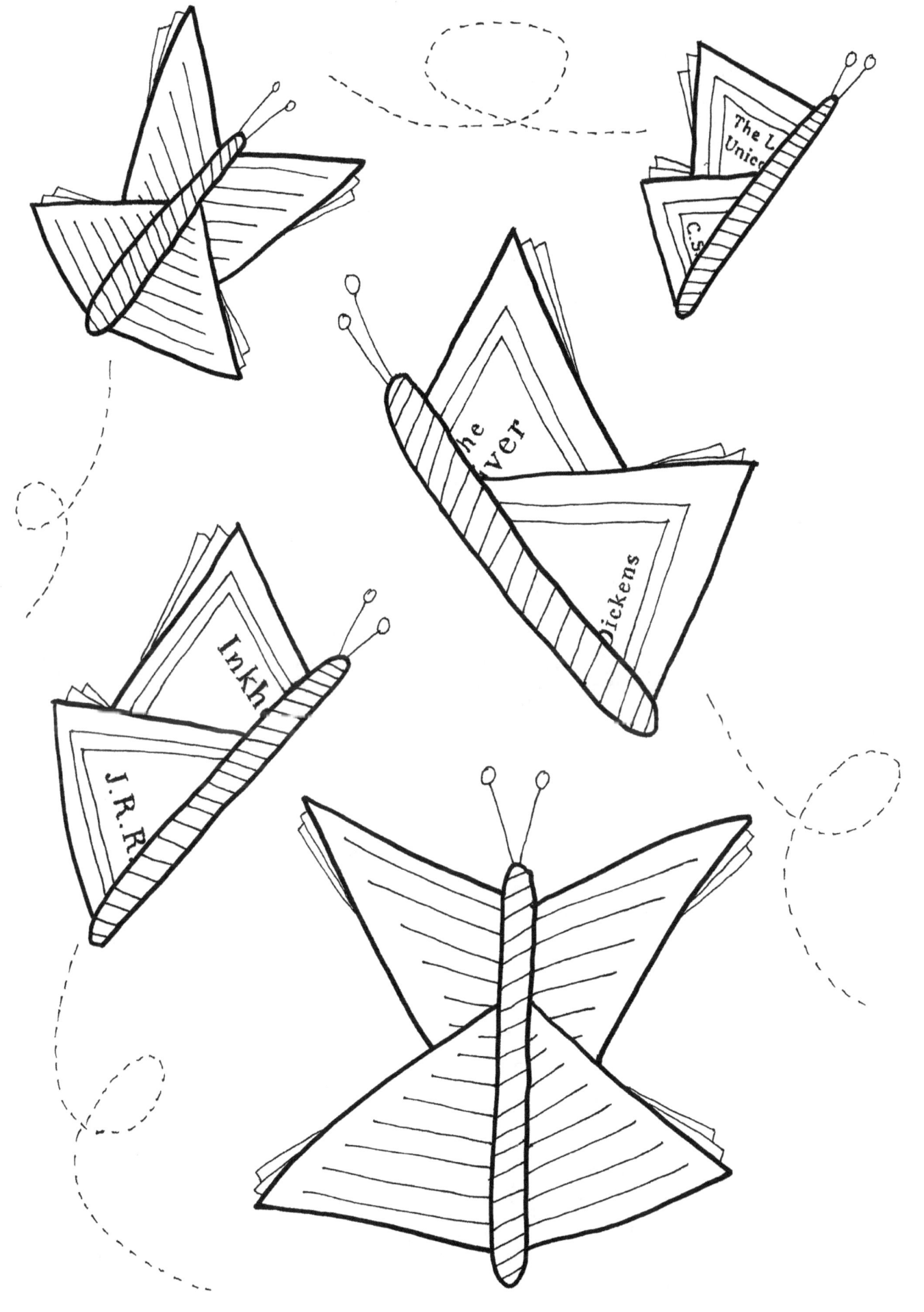

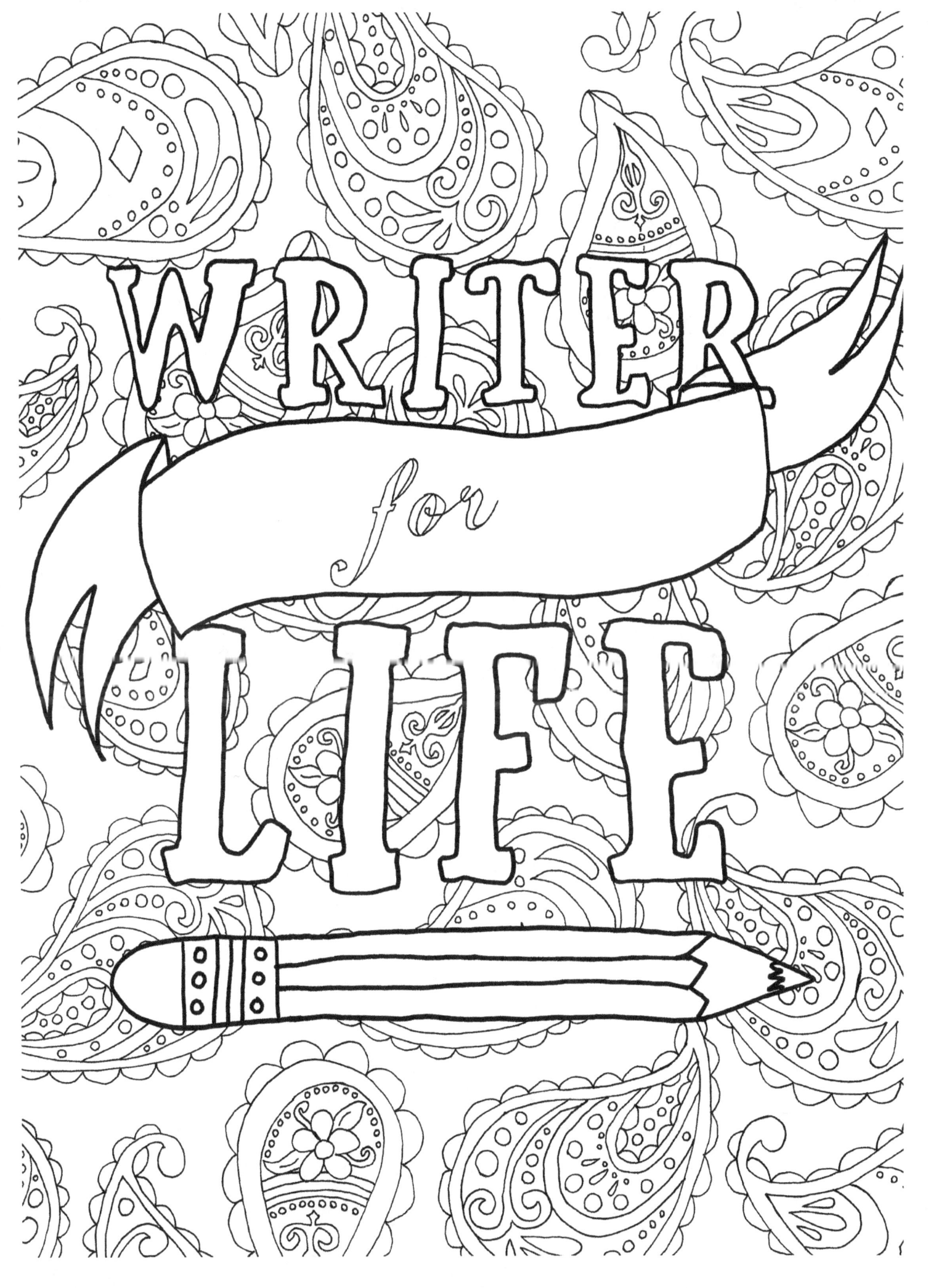

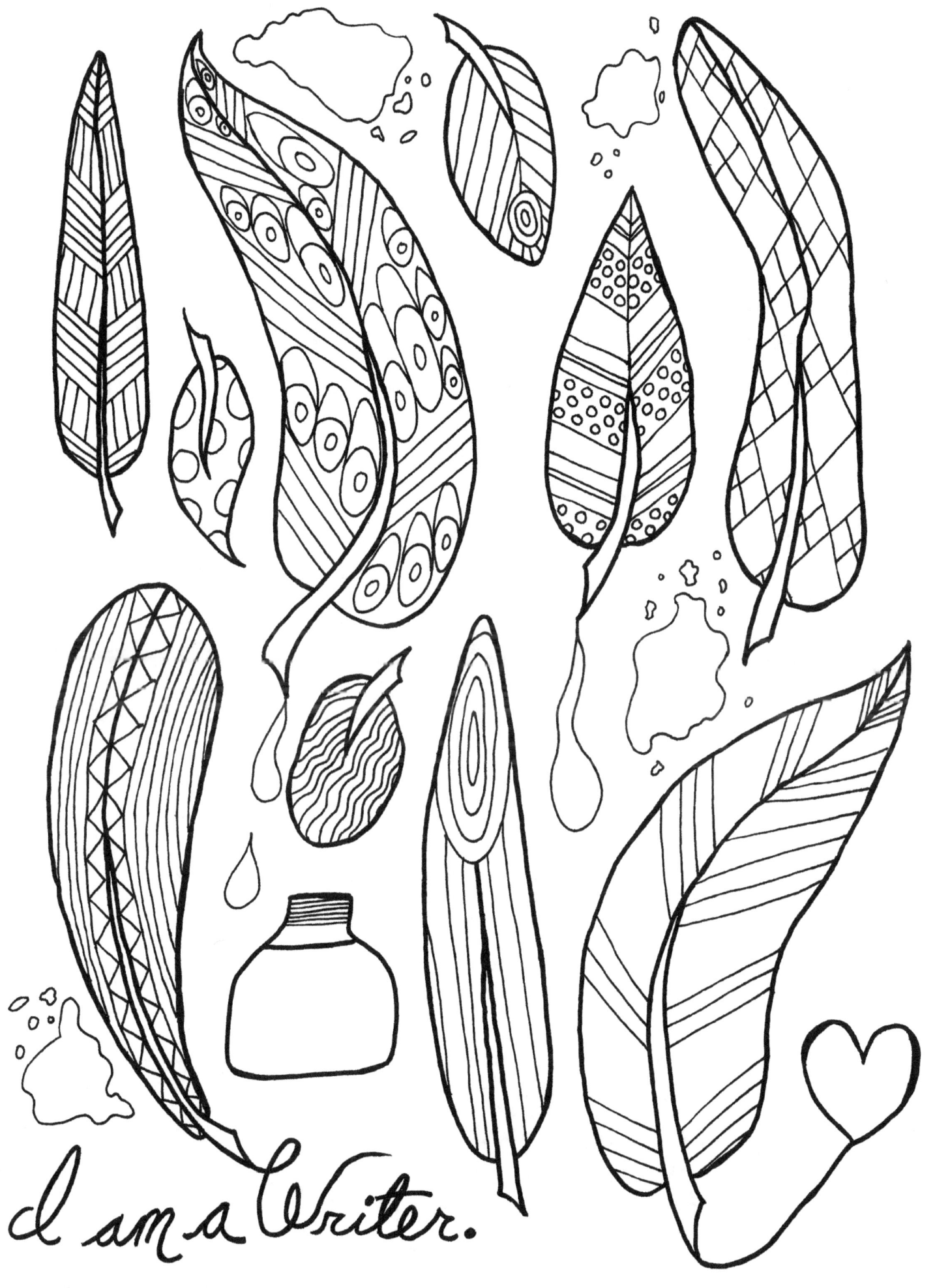

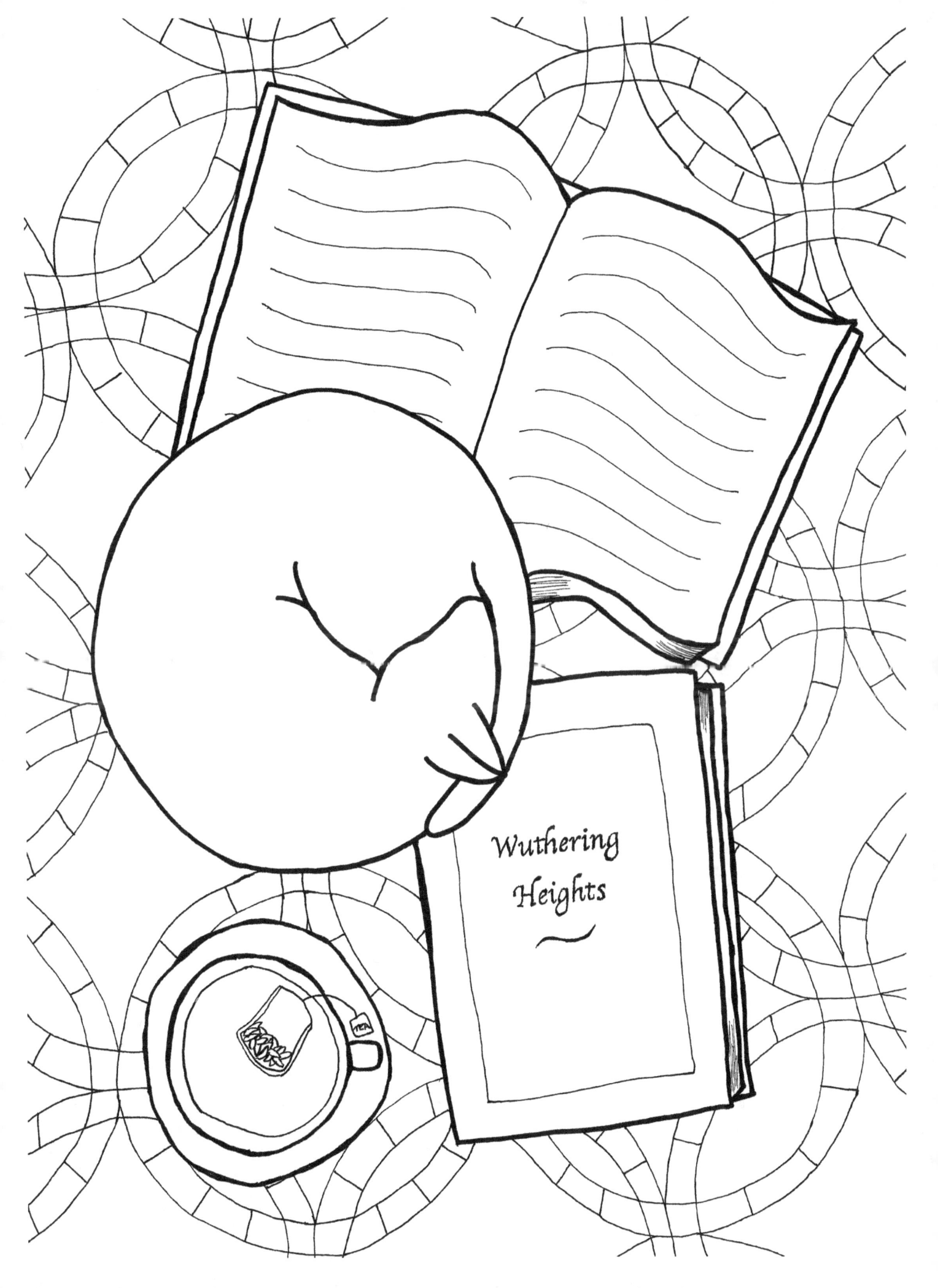

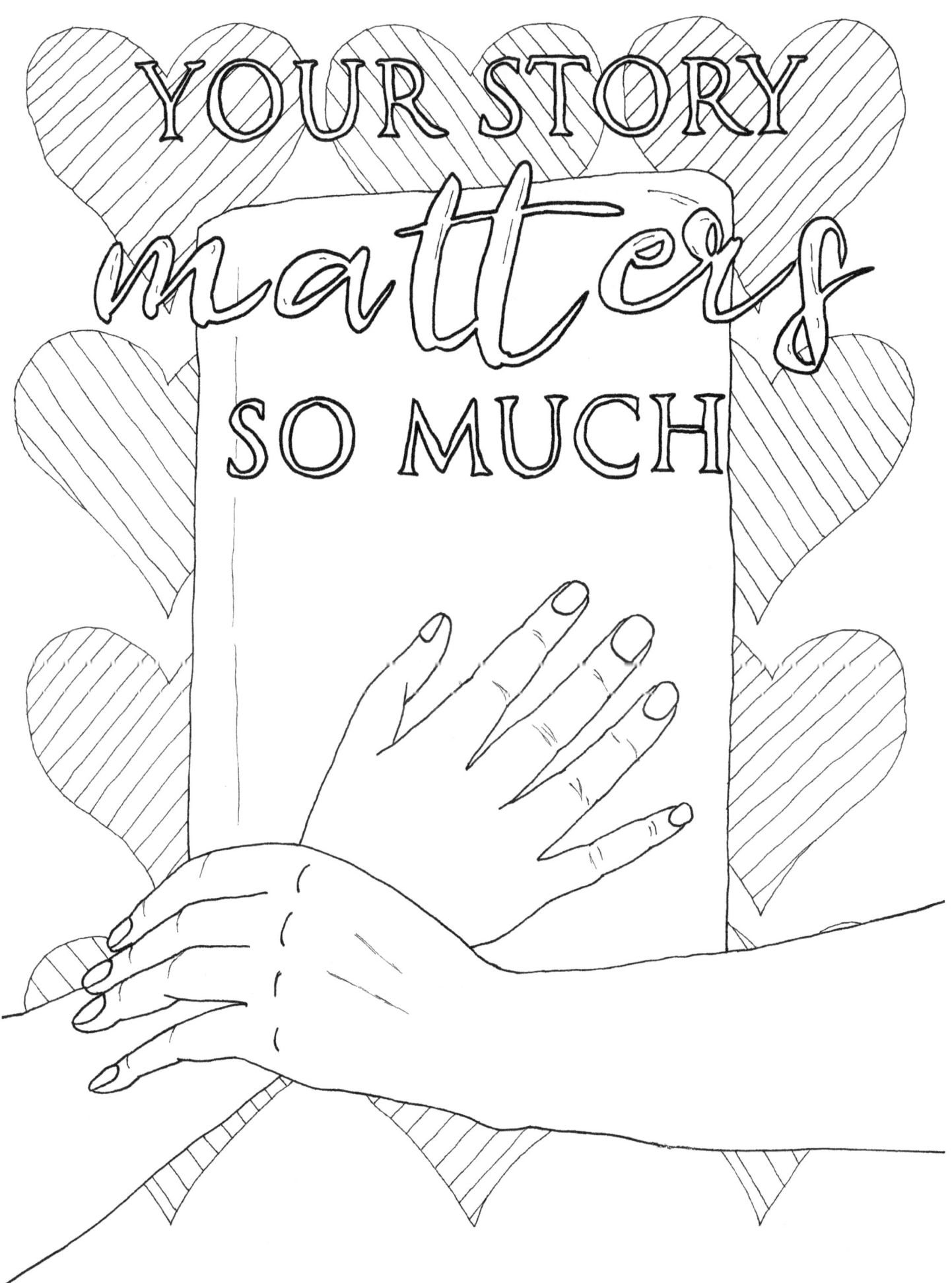

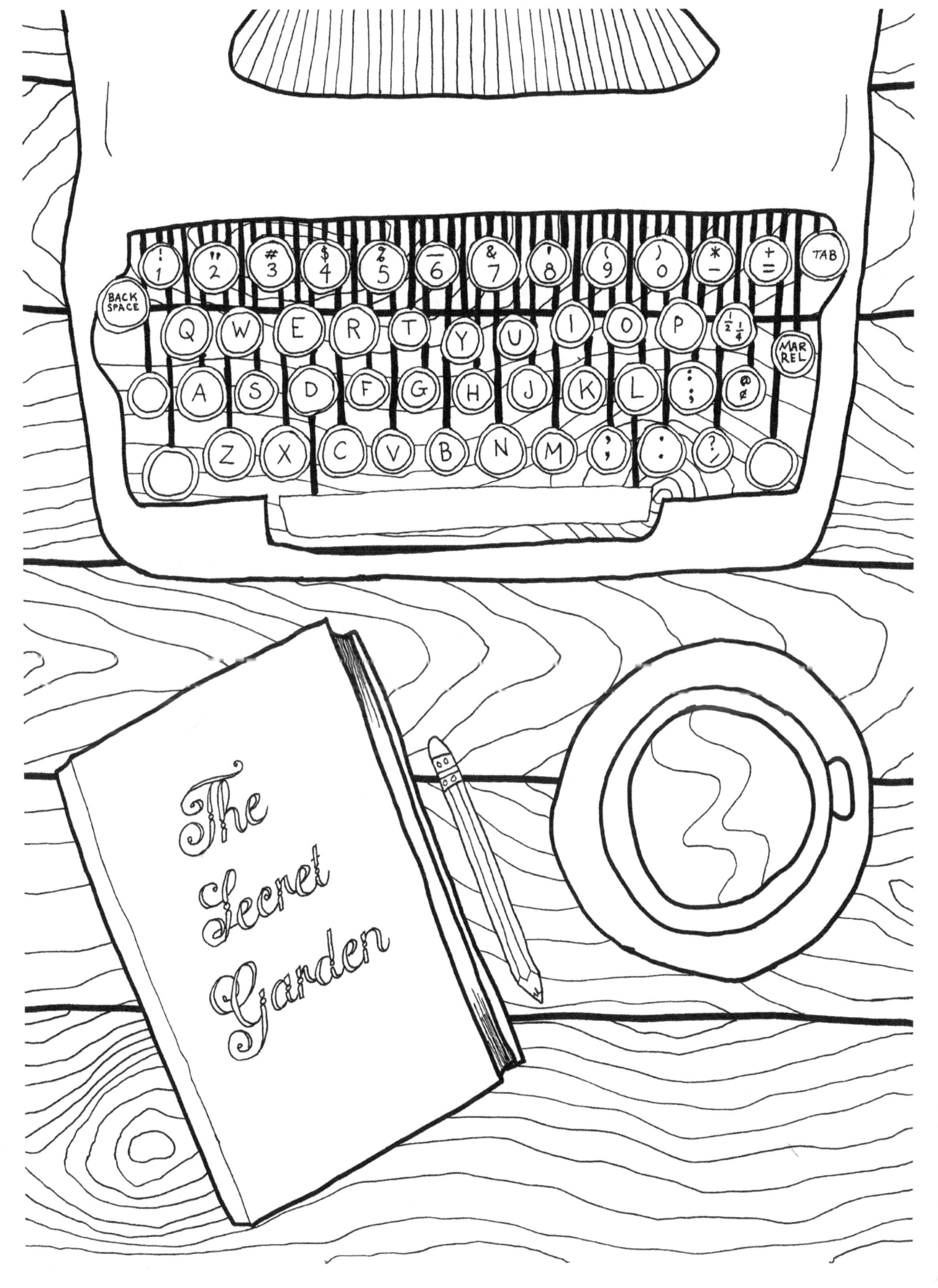

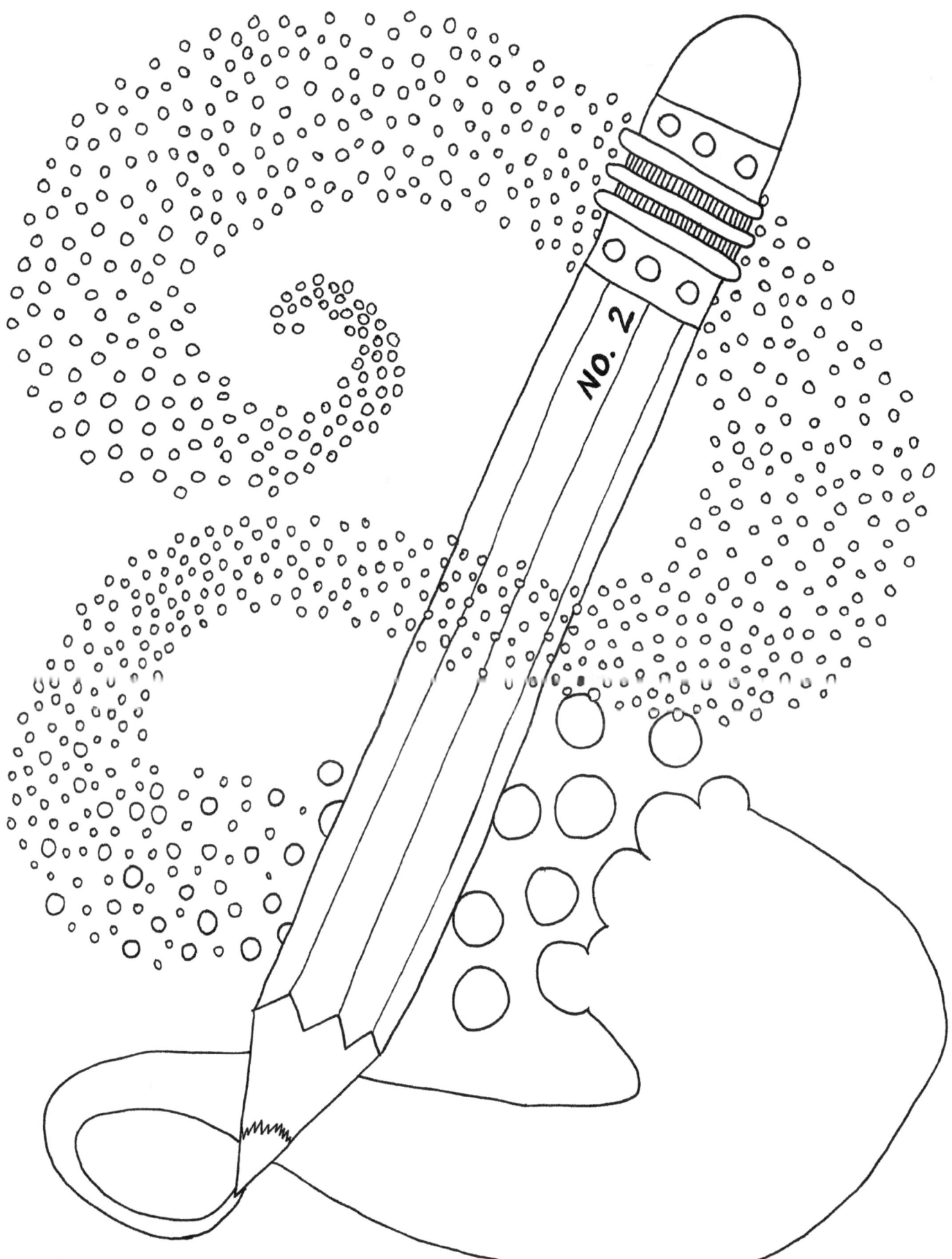

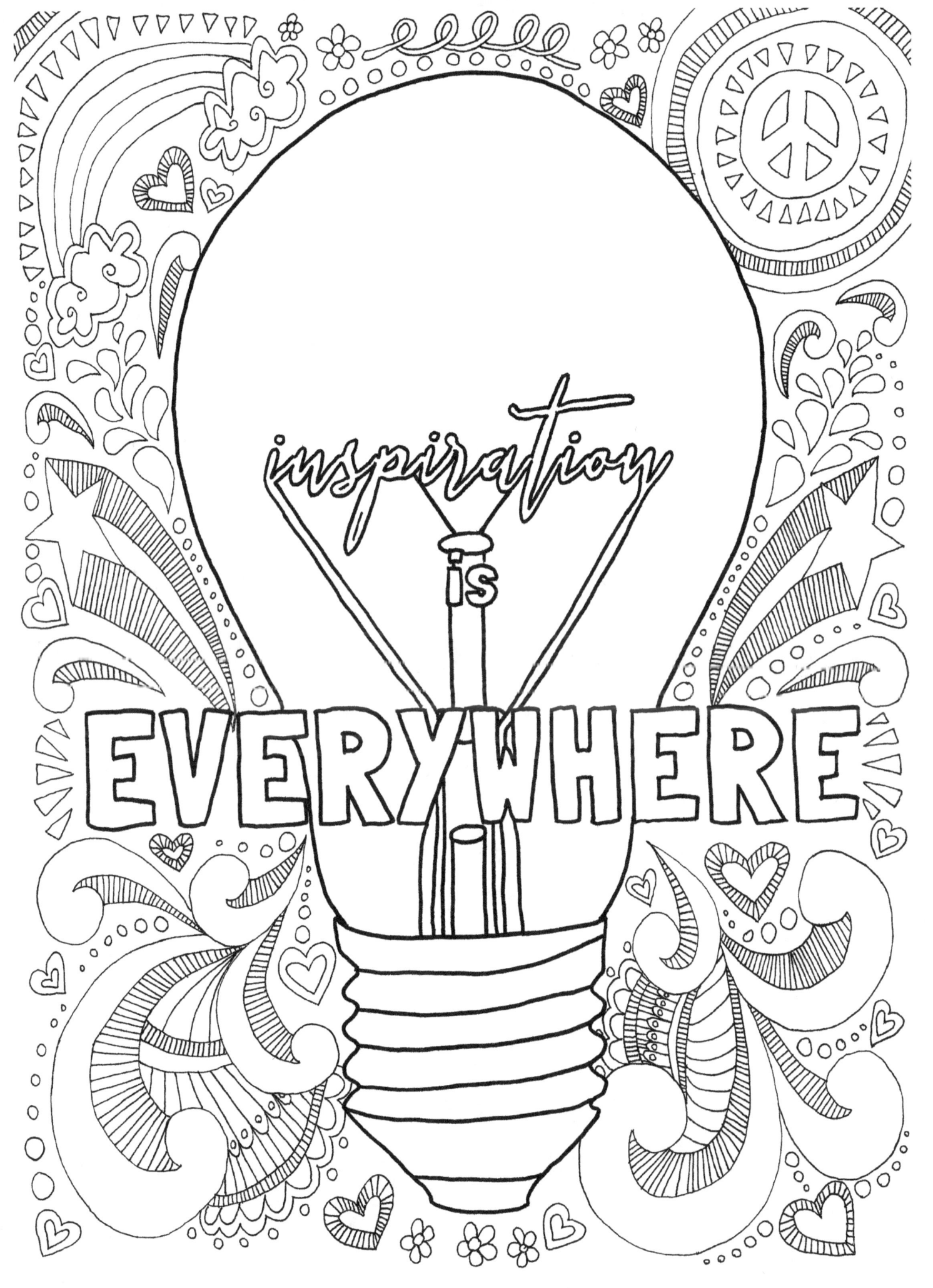

READ

I ♥ BOOKS

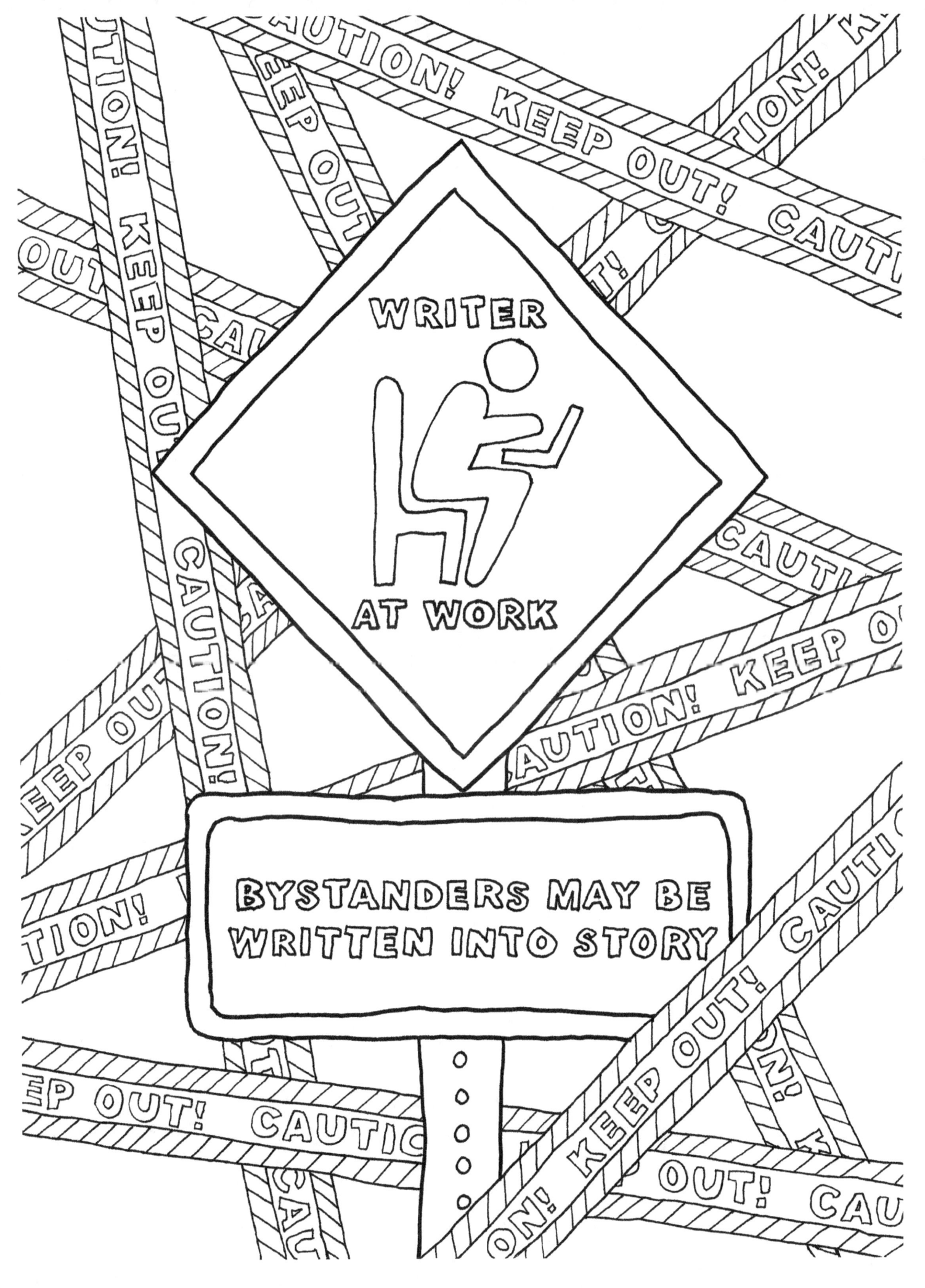

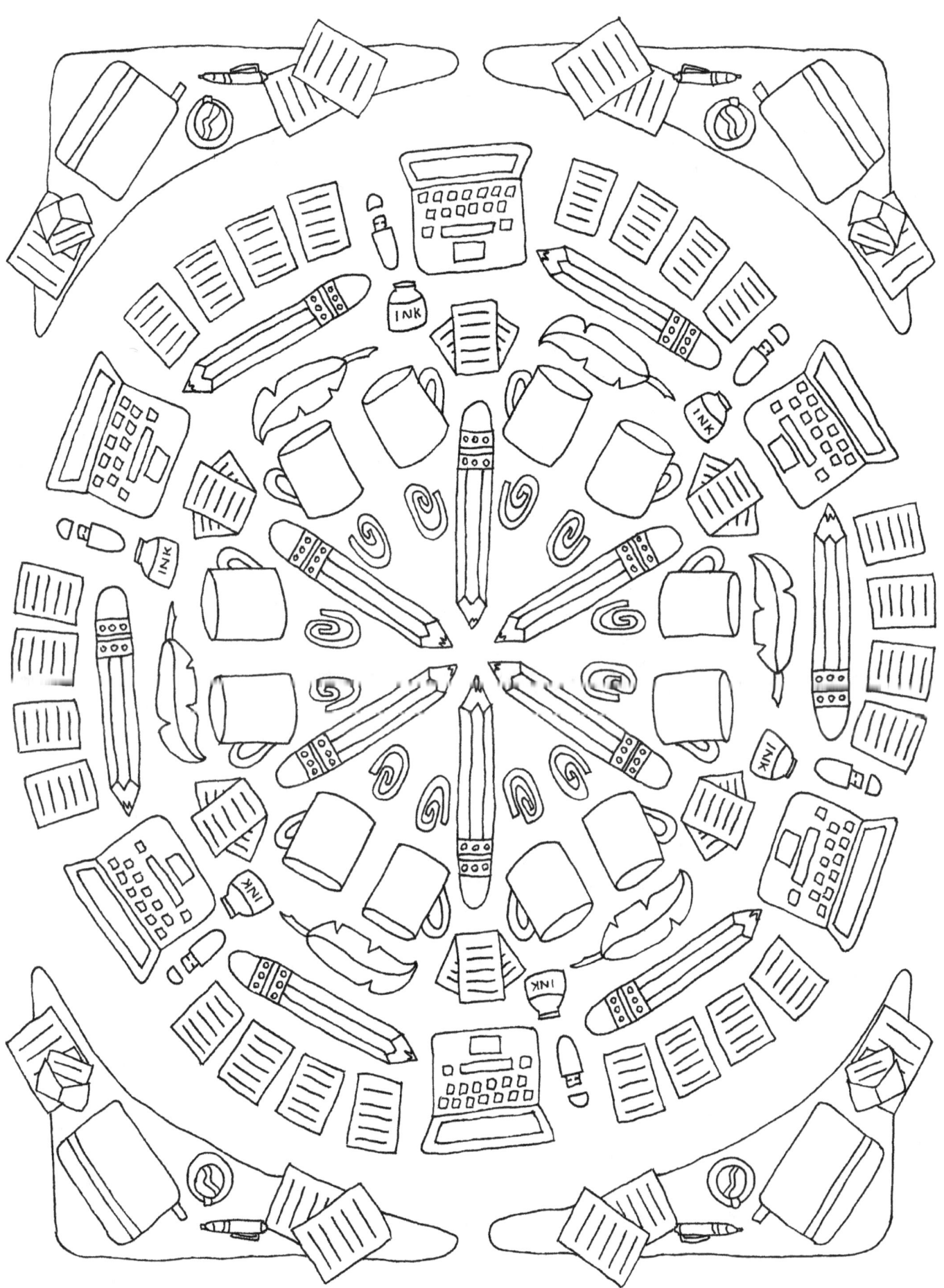

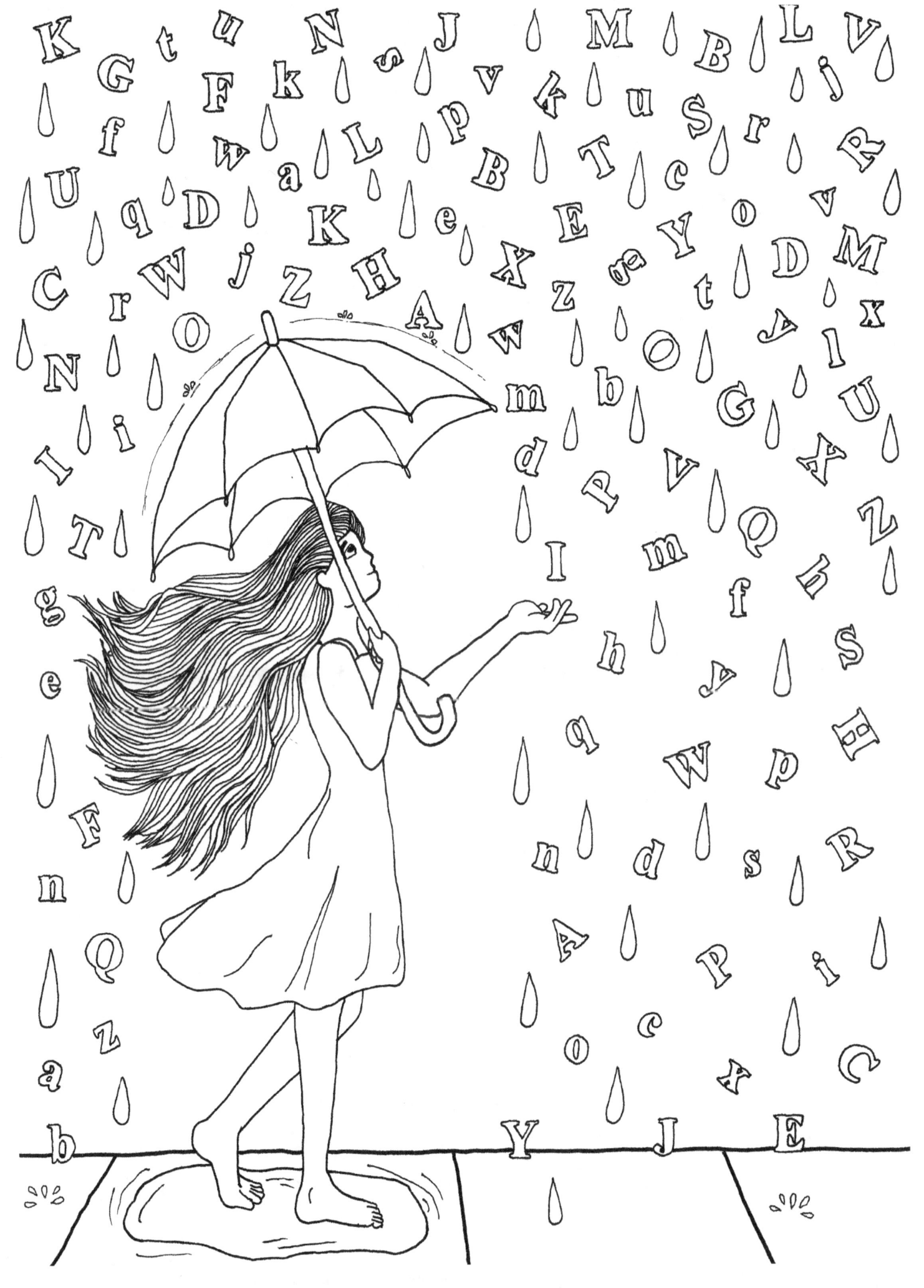

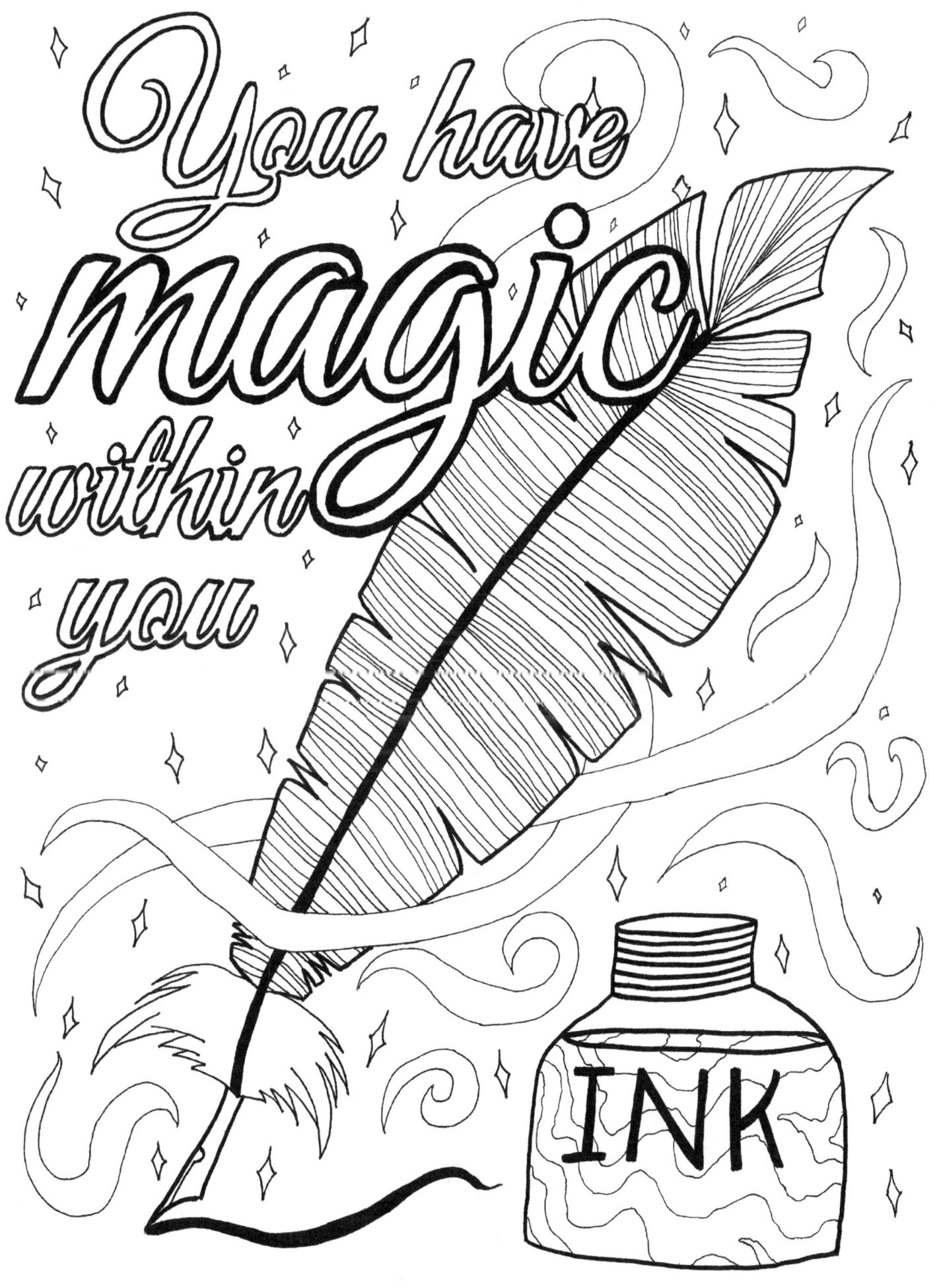

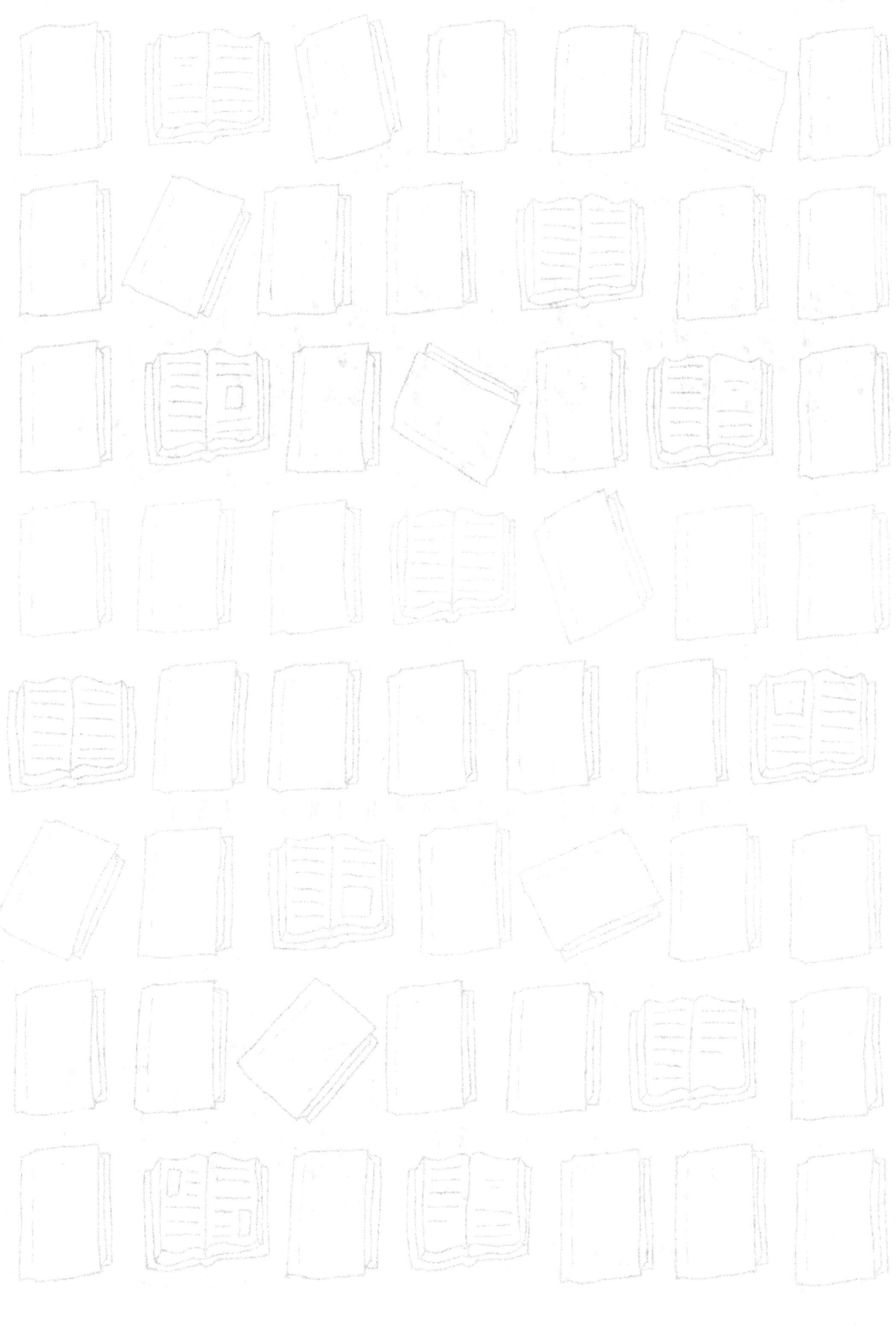

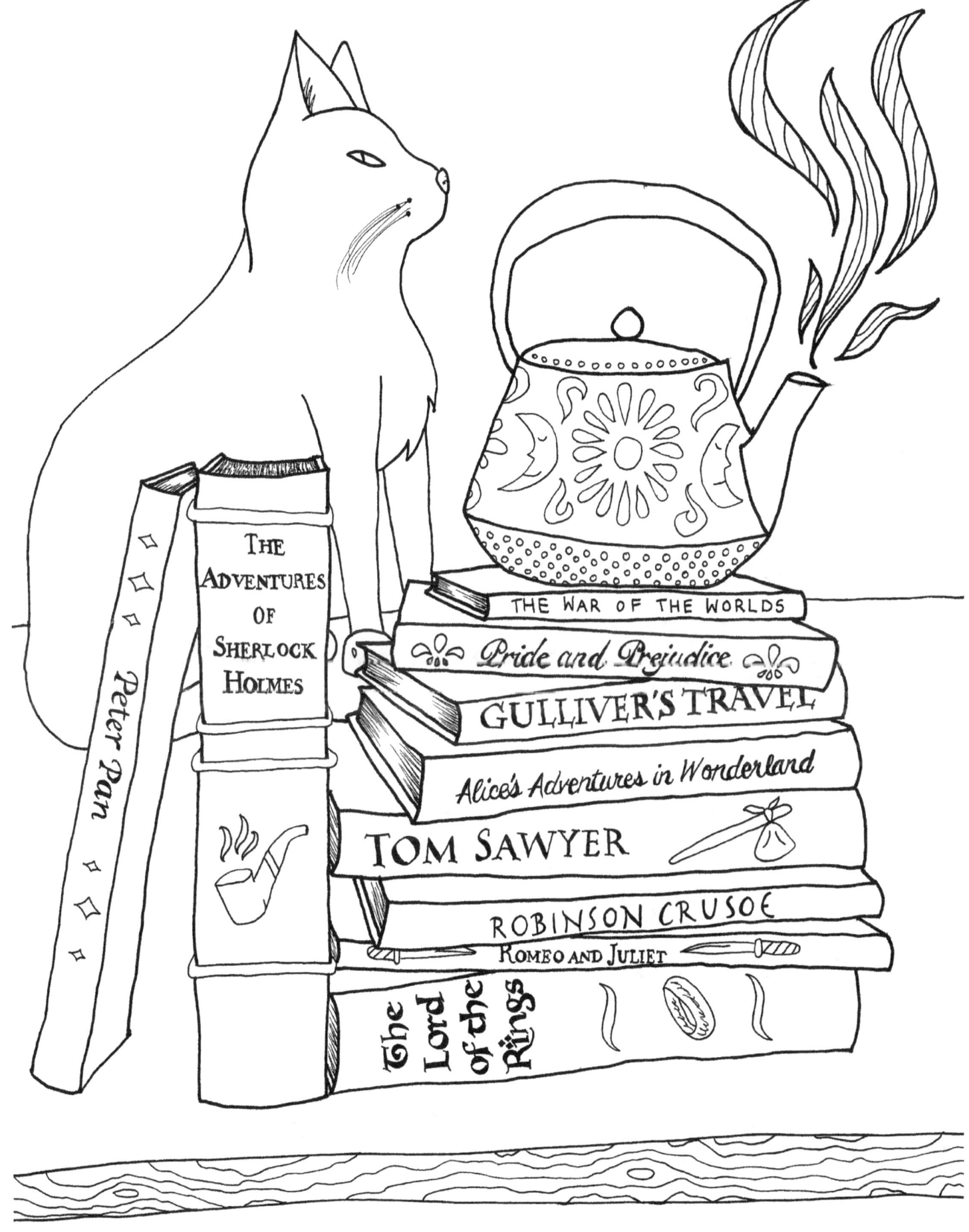

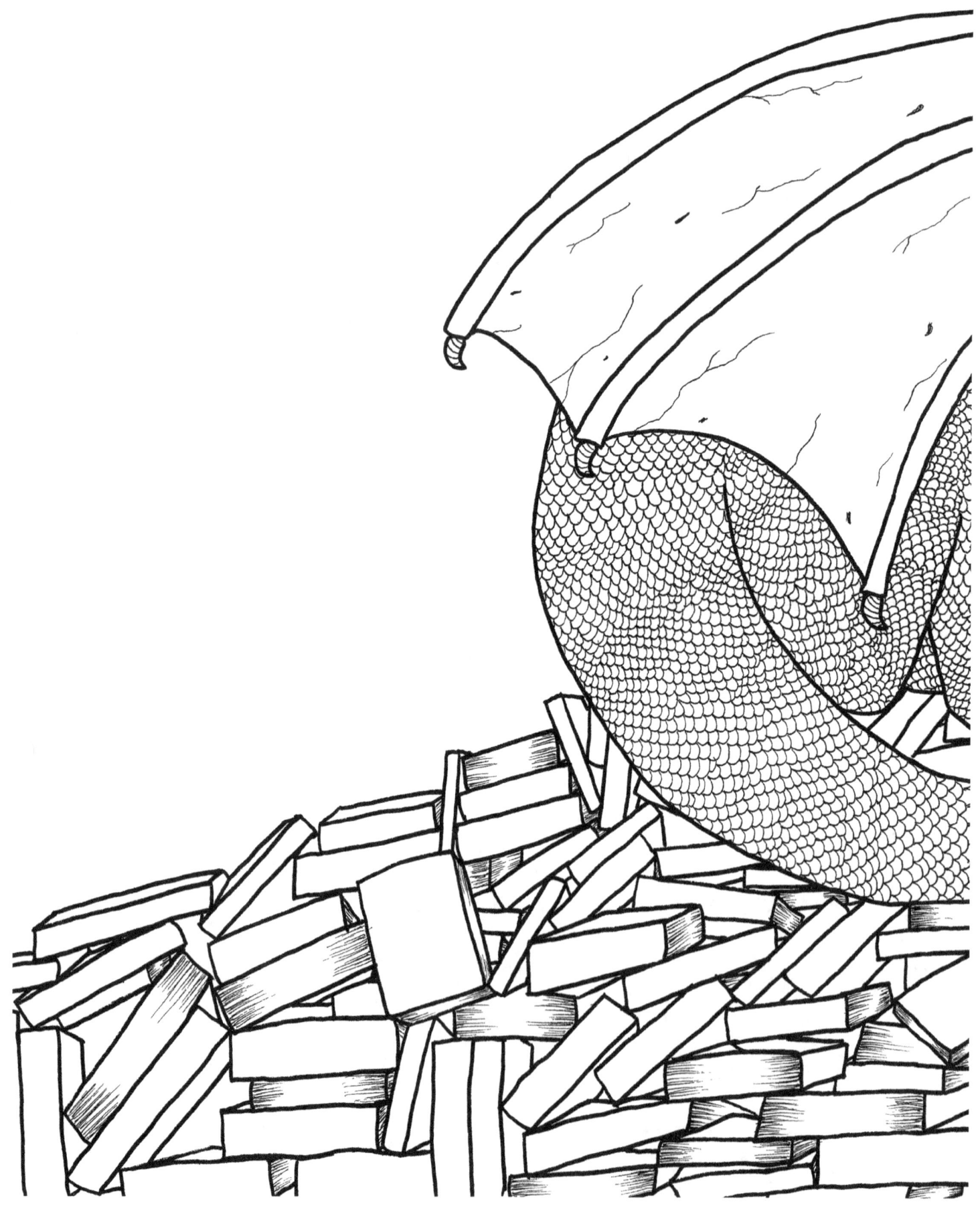

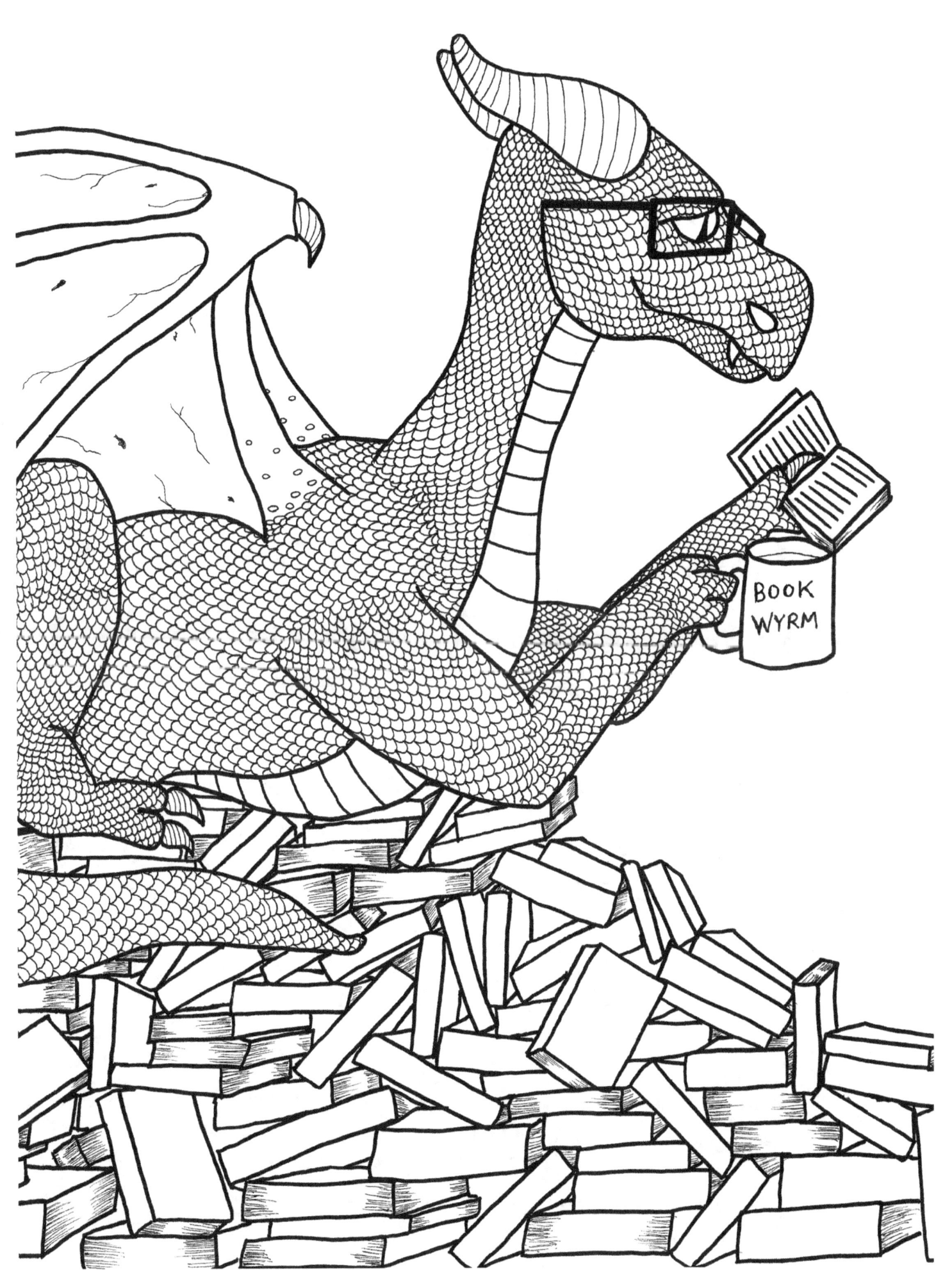

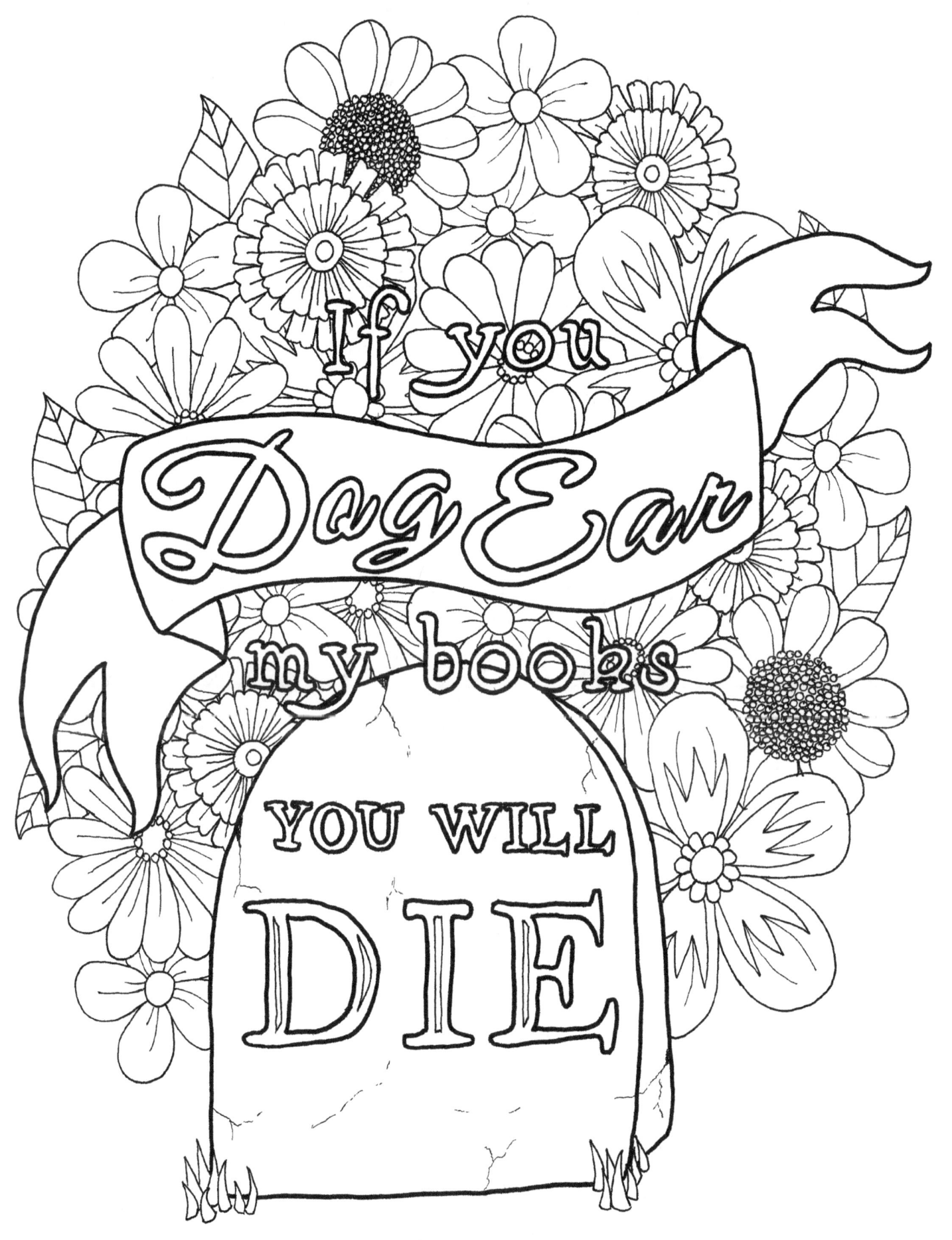

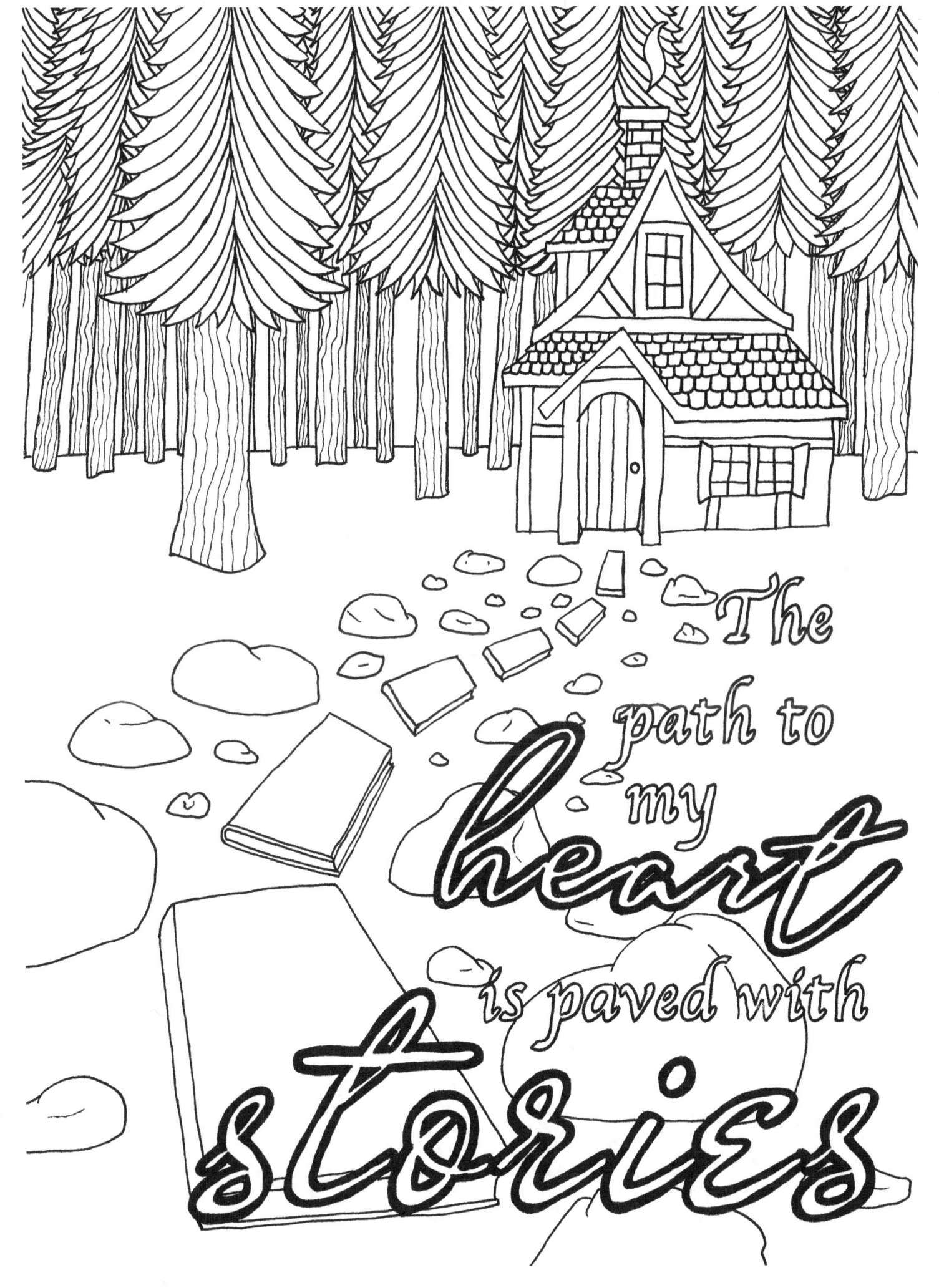

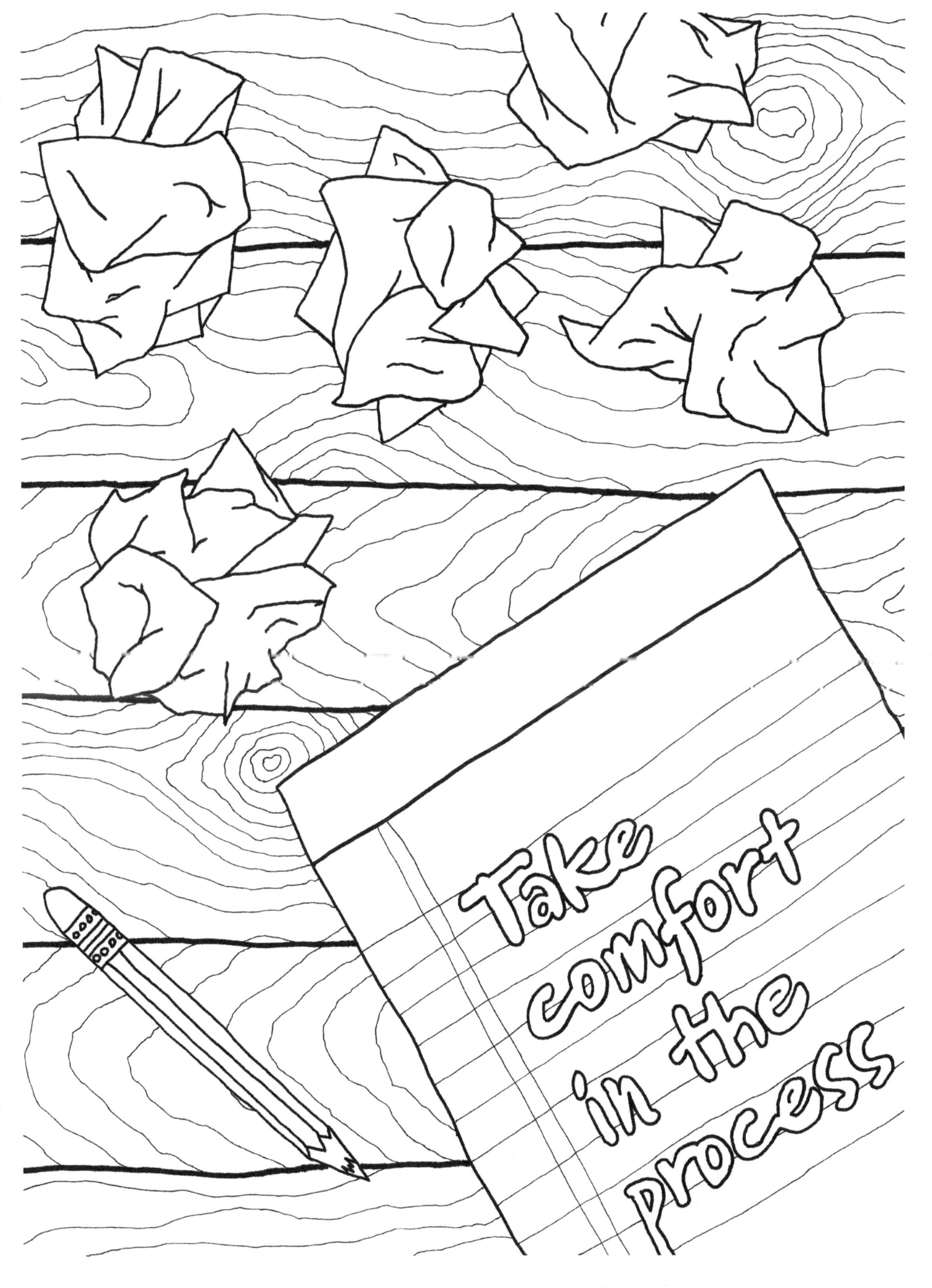

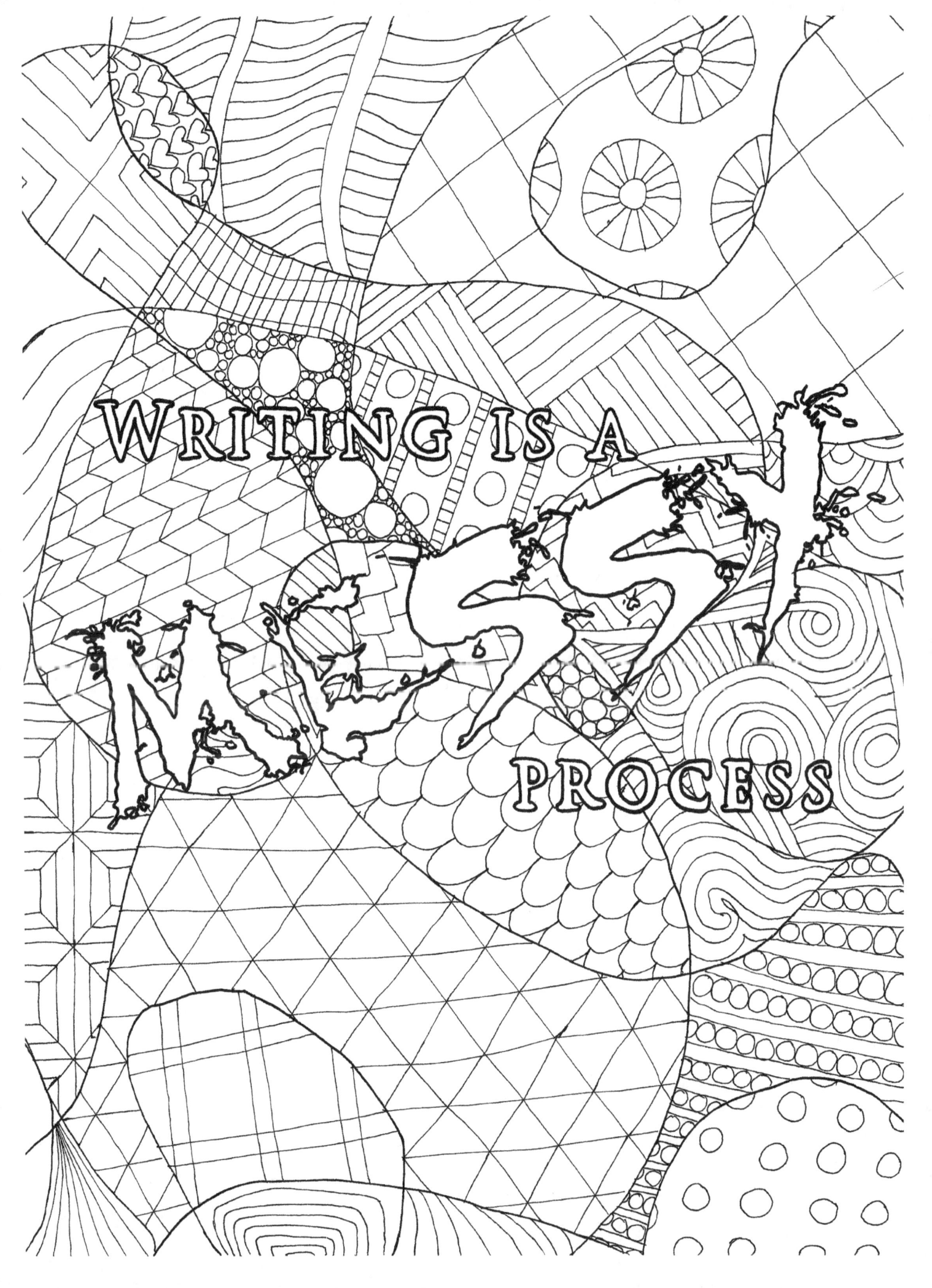

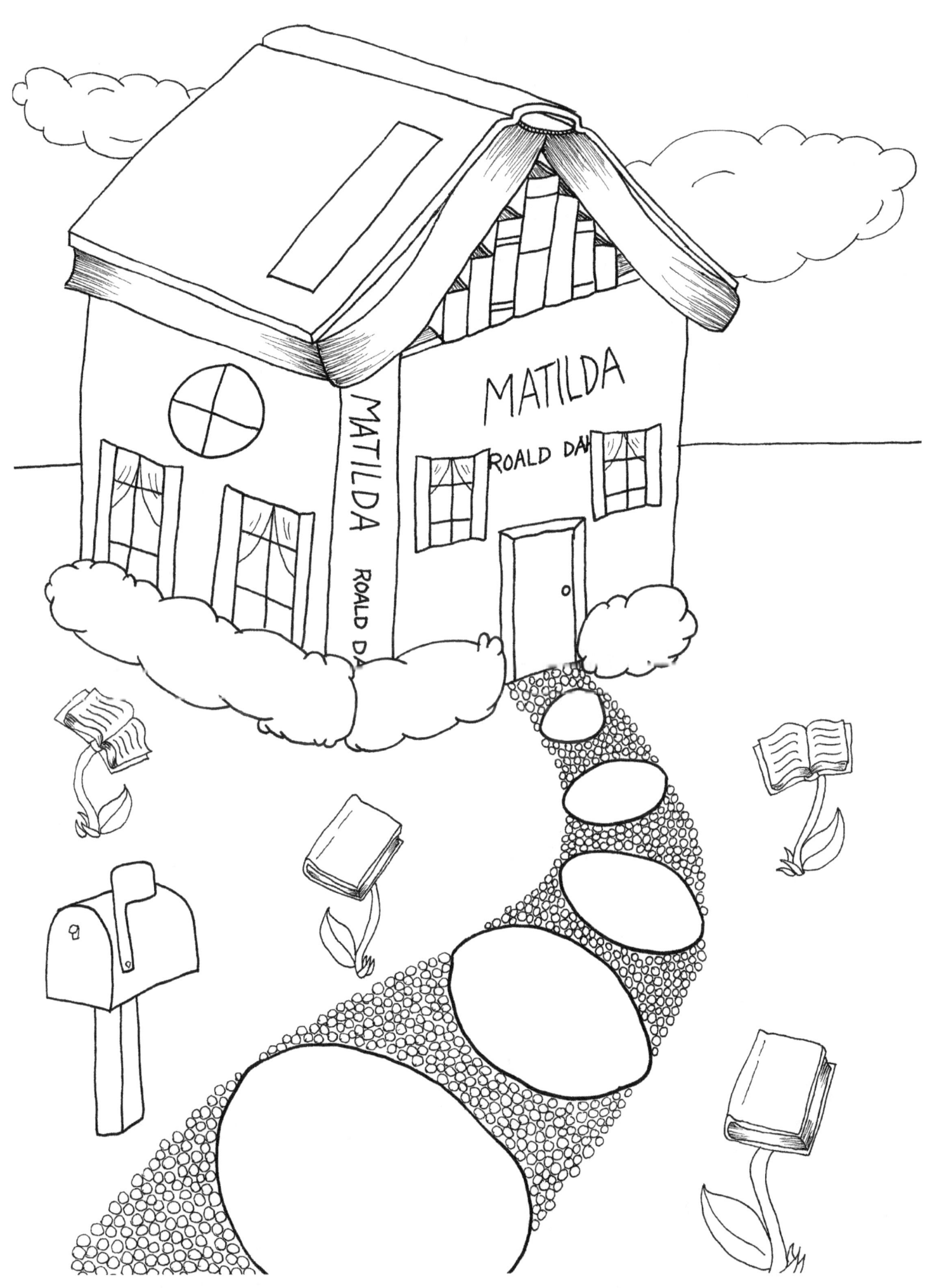

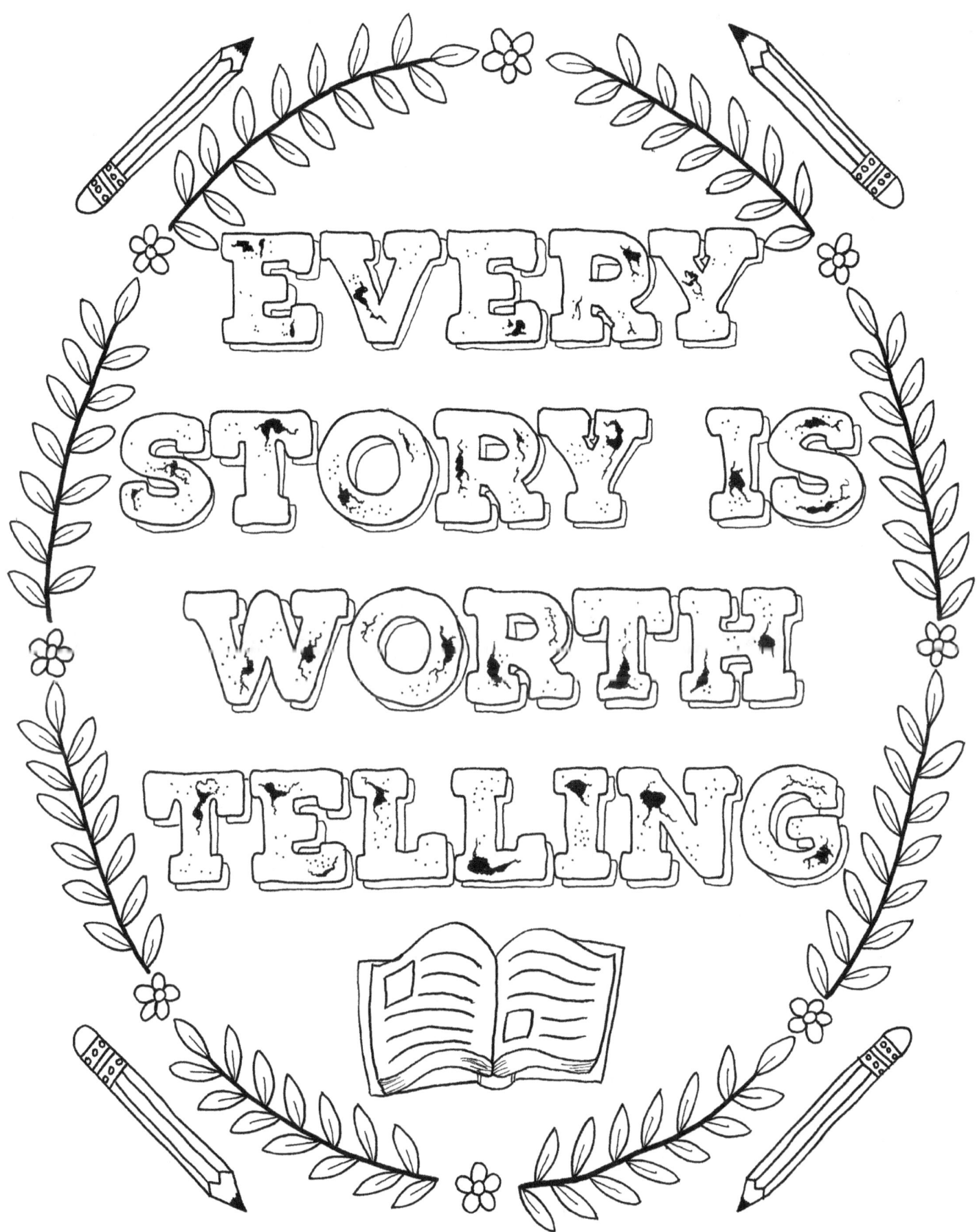

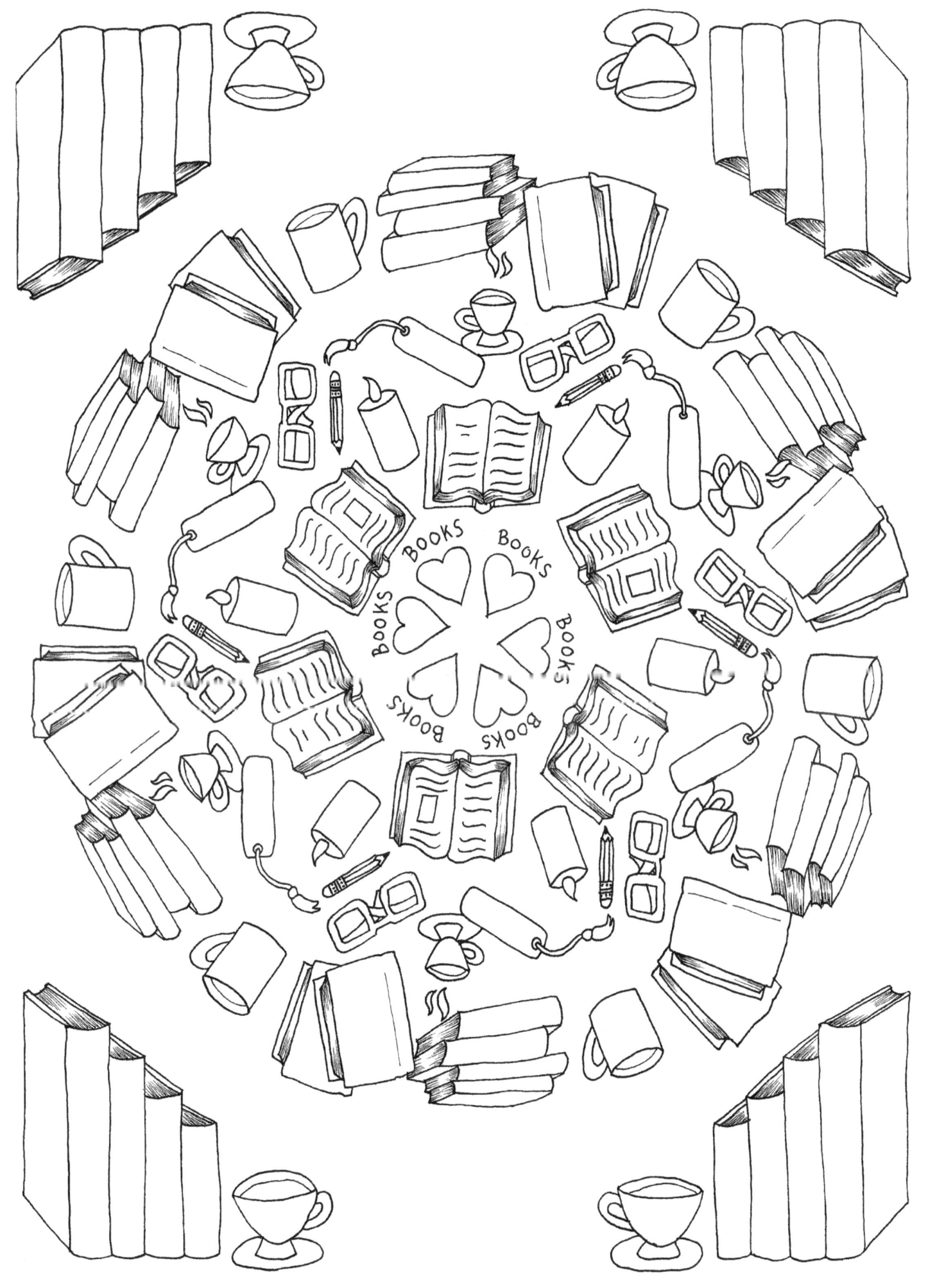

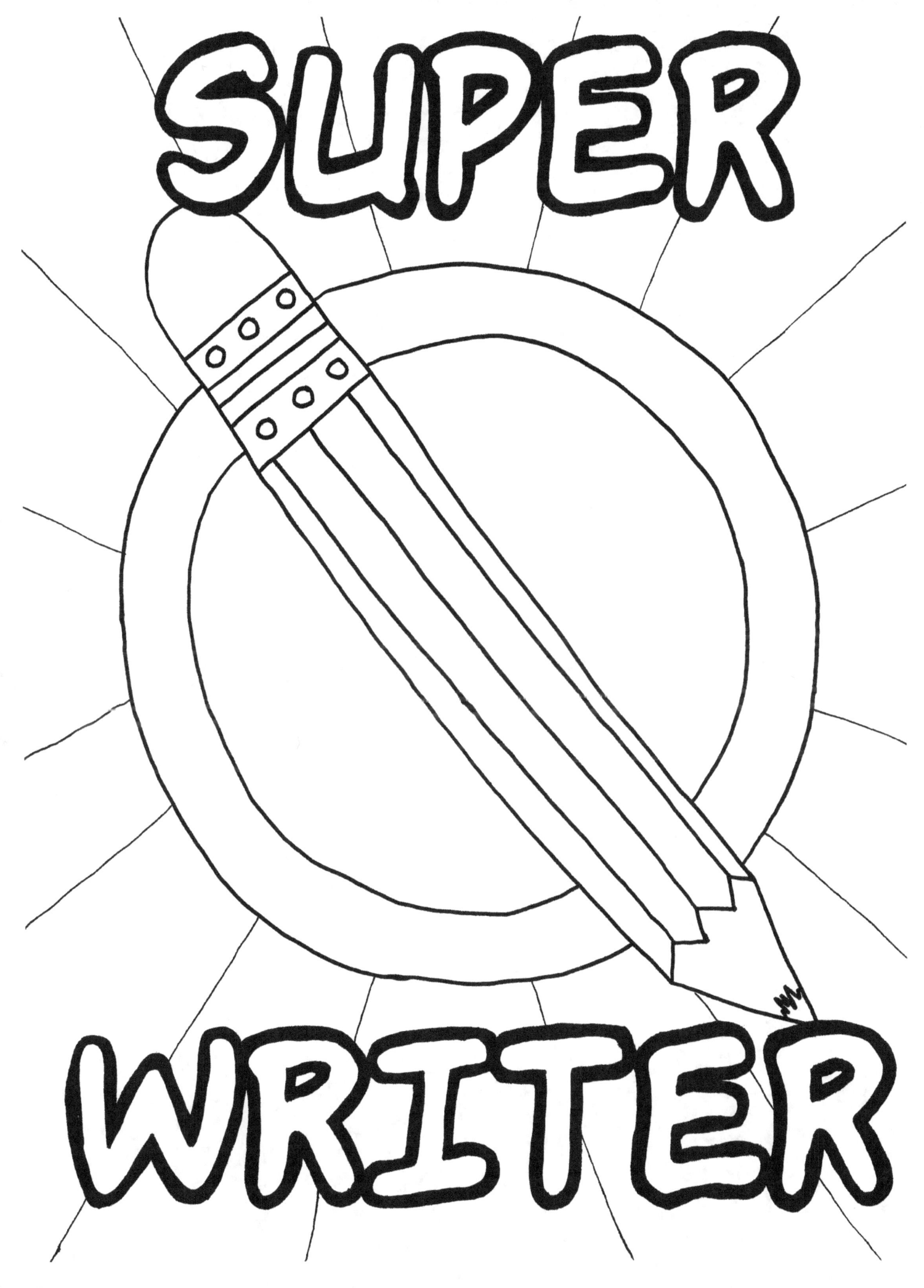

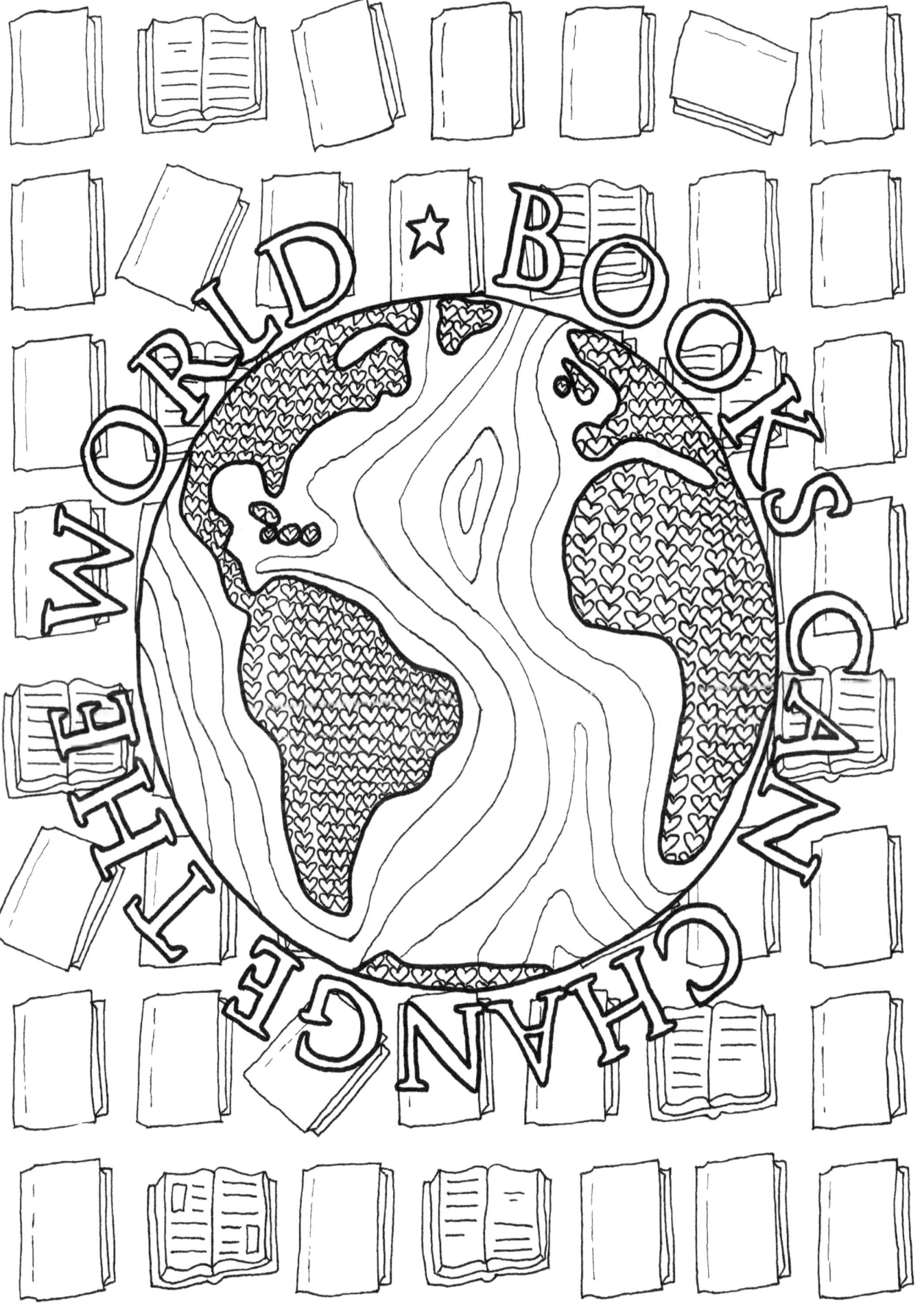

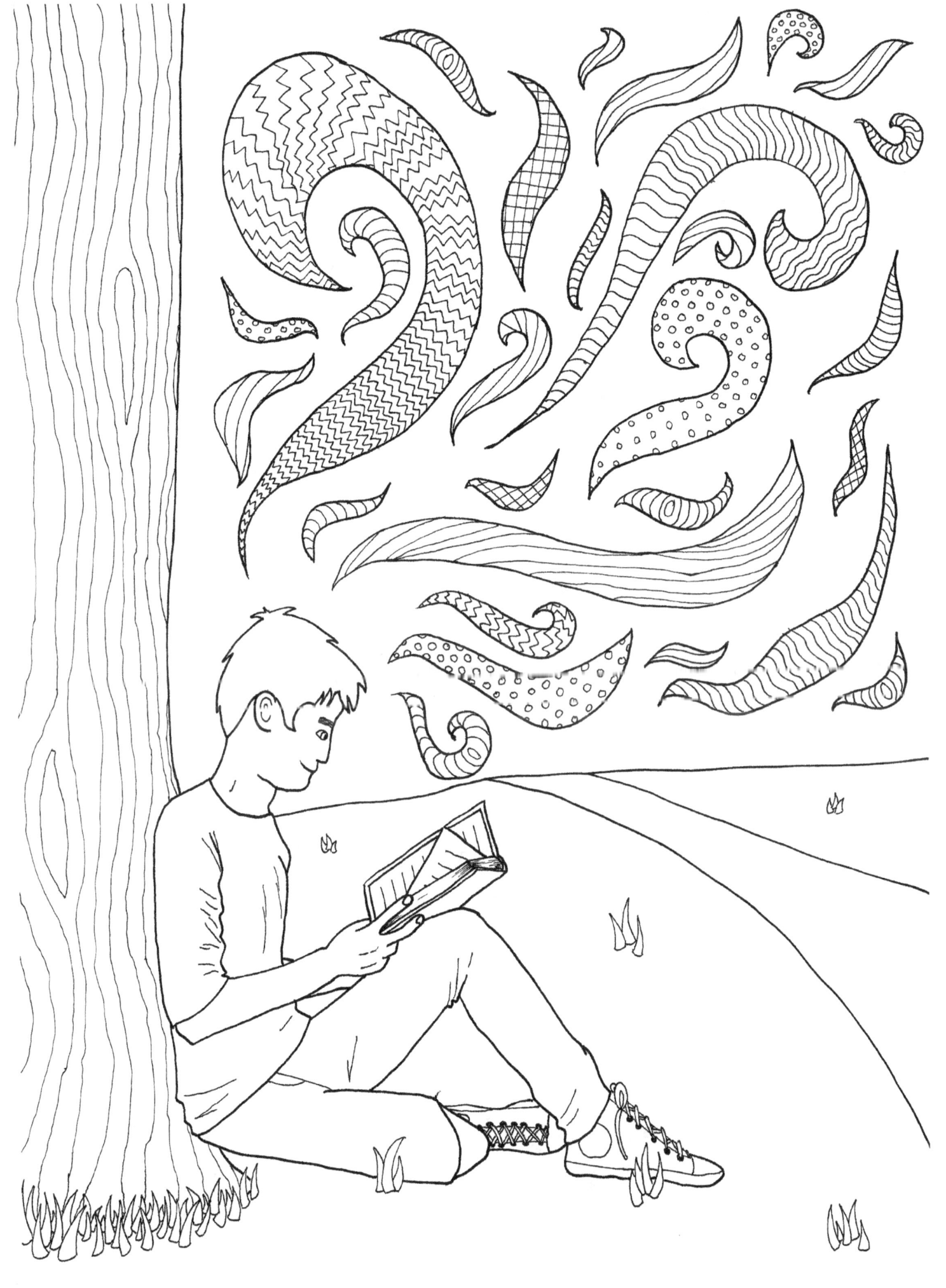

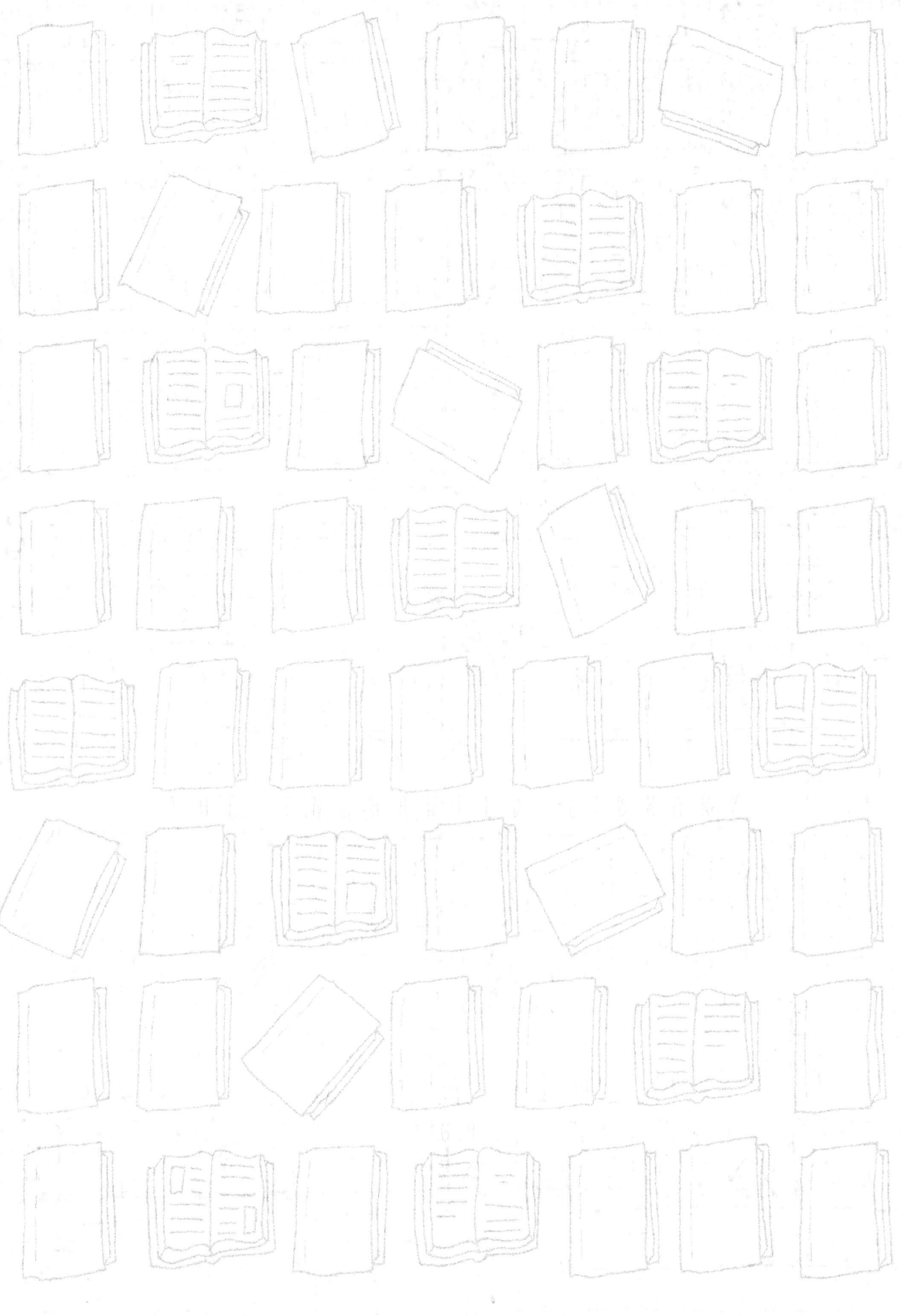

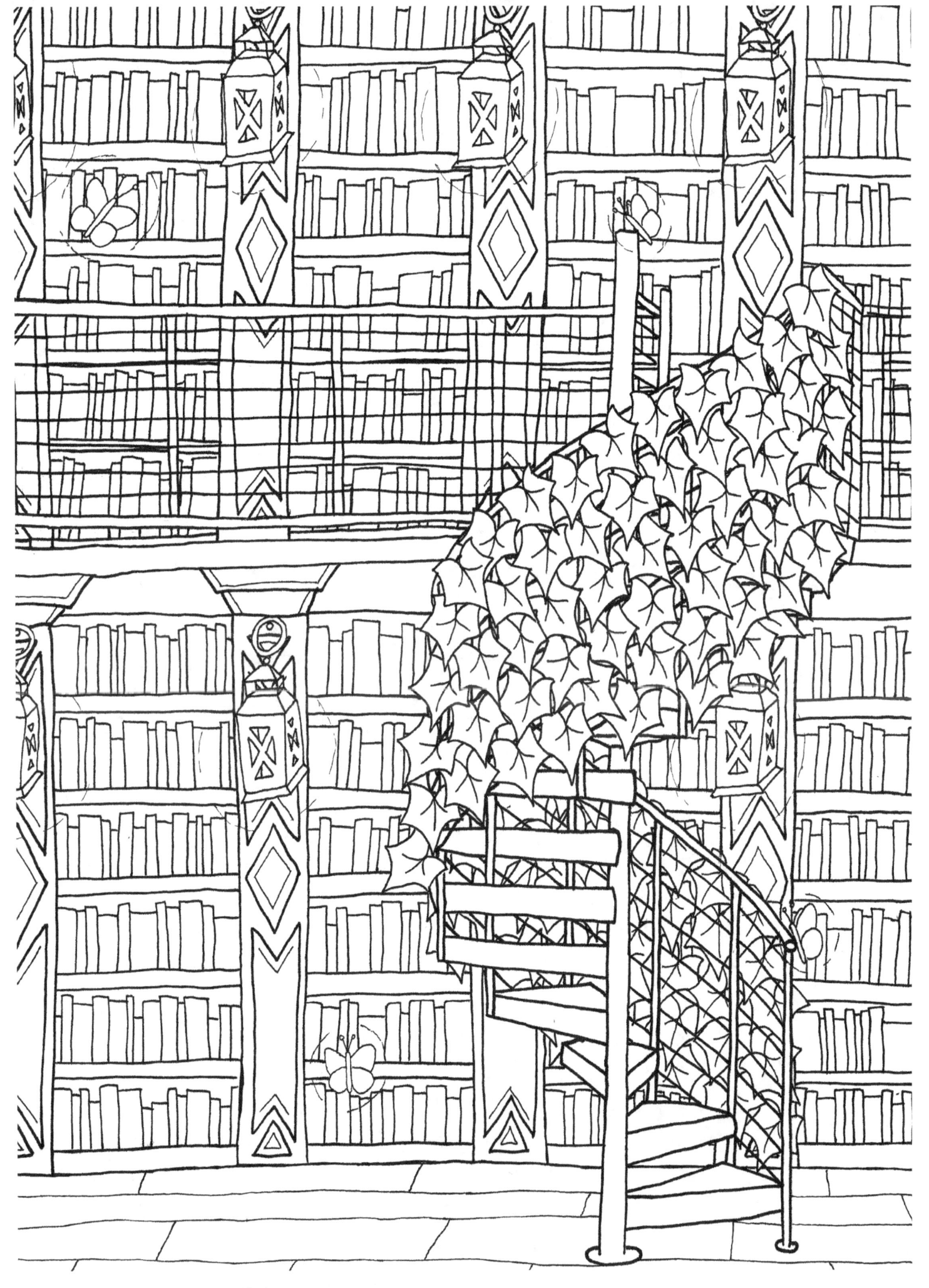

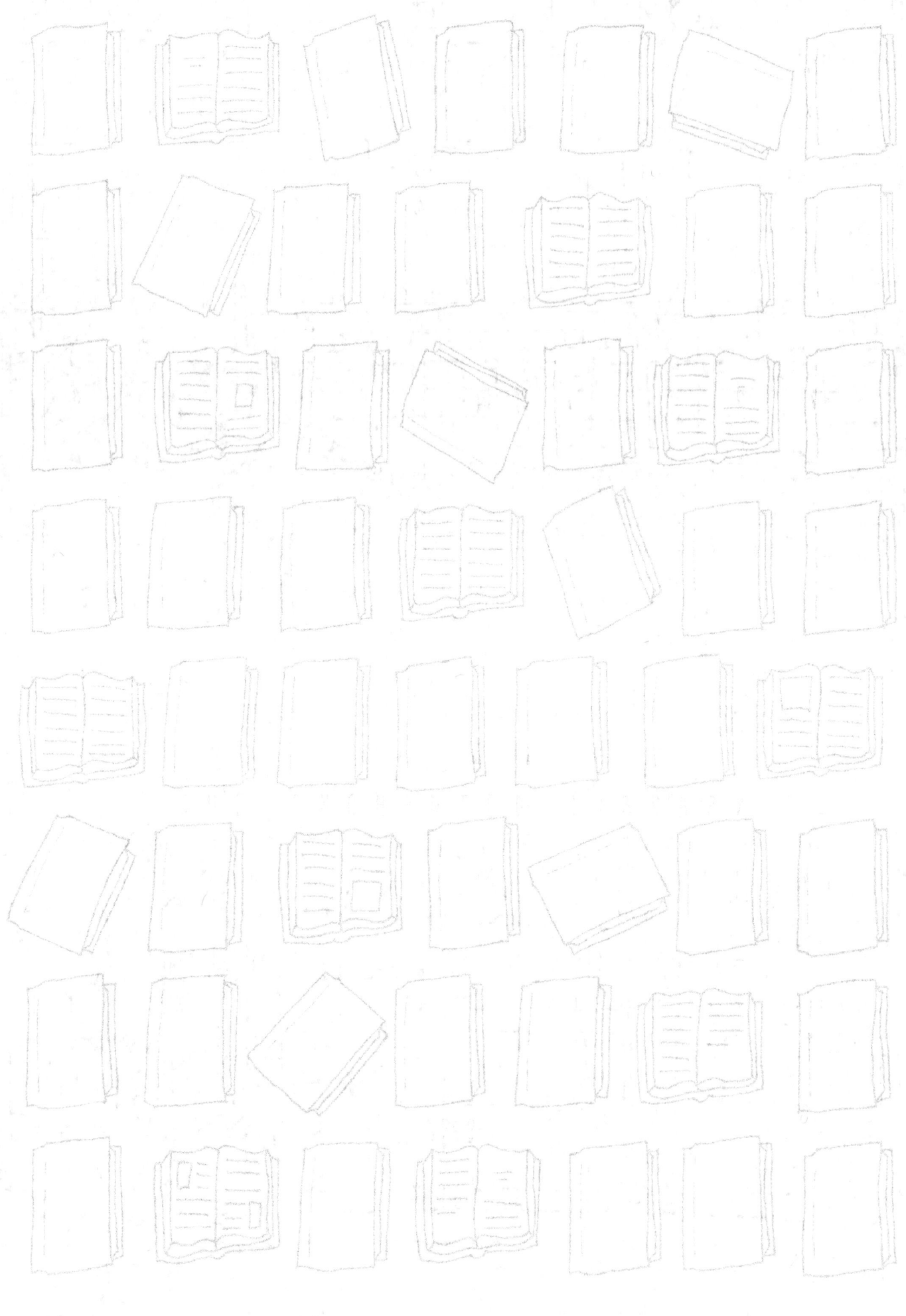

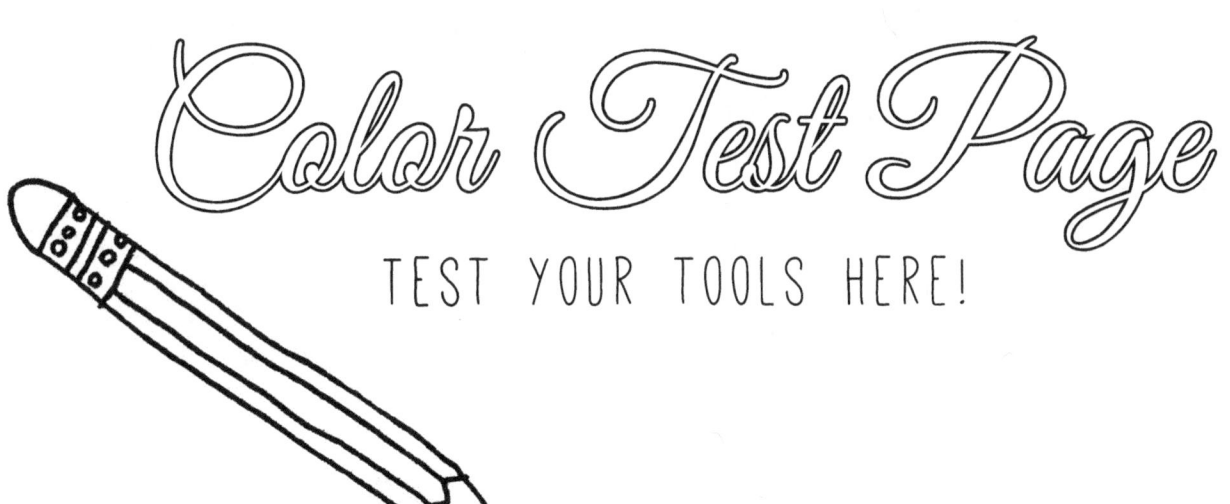
Color Test Page
TEST YOUR TOOLS HERE!